GAMES *Psychics* PLAY

A GUIDEBOOK TO ENHANCE YOUR INTUITIVE AND PSYCHIC GIFTS

KASS HILLARD

FRANKLIN ROSE
PUBLISHING

ISBN: 978-1-7247296-0-3 (Paperback)

ISBN: 978-1-7347296-1-0 (eBook)

Library of Congress Control Number: 2020914098

CONTENTS

To Spirit - every day it is my deepest desire to touch the face of God. I am grateful to do so.

To my husband, Rob - your unwavering love and belief in me give me strength. You are my beloved.

To my children, Chris, Kali, Benjamin, and Torrion - you are my heart; my most desired dreams come true. Because I always tell you to do what you're afraid of, I had to find the courage to write this book. You are the best parts of me.

ACKNOWLEDGEMENTS:

Thank you to my wonderful team of cheerleaders: Kathy Conder, Echo Bodine, Pam Me-La Martin, and Christina Thompson. Your encouragement to always keep going helped me to move forward when I wanted to stop. You are my cherished friends. To Mom and Jody, my cheerleaders in Spirit. You've always believed in me. I hope I've made you proud.

So much appreciation goes out to Amy Vos and Becky Flansburg for their suggestions to make this book better, and Kali Adriantje for her wordsmanship and mad editing skills. Thank you, Alyson Gannon and Franklin Rose Publishing, for giving me this opportunity.

And thank you to the individuals who have attended my development classes over the years. I've learned so much from you all.

INTRODUCTION

"AUNT RUTH IS COMING OVER," I announced to my mom late one Sunday morning.

"What makes you think so?"

"It just feels like it," and off I went to play.

Two hours later, Aunt Ruth and my two cousins (who lived 90 miles away) pulled into our driveway. My mom looked at me in disbelief.

I was six or seven and this was the first time I consciously remember having a psychic premonition. My mom didn't know what to do with a child who "knew things," so she ignored it.

Growing up, I would hear voices at night when I was lying in bed. They sounded loud but muffled and I couldn't make out what they were saying. It seemed the more I tried to ignore them, the louder they got. This terrified me. I would pull the covers over my head to try to make the voices stop. What did they want from me? What were they trying to say?

Spirit, oftentimes, would visit me in my dreams. I felt a certain comfort, when my deceased grandmother, who died months before I was born, visited in this way. Was I imagining this?

These experiences continued into adulthood.

One morning, while on a house call, I heard my mom call out my name. I turned to answer her, but she wasn't there. And why would she be? I was at work and she was at home. Upon returning home several hours later, I learned my mom had died that morning…at approximately the same time I'd heard my name called.

Sitting alone on the wooden stage of a darkened theater, during a paranormal investigation, I was anxious to try my new in-real-time recorder. Wondering and hoping I'd get some evidence, I turned the recorder on and asked, "who's here?"

"I'm here" was the whispered reply. Shocked to hear an immediate response, I didn't think to ask who it was, but I knew. It was my mom. And this was the eve of her death anniversary.

As a child, I didn't have answers to my questions about these and similar occurrences, and worse yet, there was no one I could ask. This is the book I wish I'd had as an adult when I was beginning to learn about psychic phenomena. Maybe I wouldn't have been so afraid or felt so alone or different.

THOUGHTS FOR CONSIDERATION:

- What was the first intuitive or psychic experience you remember having? Were you frightened by it or did it seem normal?
- As a young child, did you experience any unexplained "coincidences" or times when you just "knew" something was going to happen?
- Have there been times when you had a "feeling" about someone, whether positive or negative? Did those feelings reveal themselves to be warranted?
- Have you seen things you couldn't explain? Tell about your experiences.
- When did your interest in psychic phenomenon begin? Did an incident occur that you felt "unleashed" your psychic powers?

Psychics are ordinary people, just like you and me. They have jobs, families, and friends. They are your neighbors, doctors, grocery clerks, teachers, clergy, mechanics, and students. They experience successes and failures, as well as triumphs and challenges in their daily lives, just as the rest of us do.

Each of us is psychic to one degree or another. Our psychic faculties are natural extensions of our physical senses. Those who consider themselves psychic have learned to connect to and trust their intuition and the psychic impressions they receive. For the rest of us, our psychic senses remain dormant until we either consciously decide to engage them OR until something occurs to arouse or spontaneously awaken them such as a near-death experience (NDE). Whenever and however your psychic gifts present themselves, I hope you learn to embrace them.

There are no shortcuts to strengthening your intuition or developing your psychic abilities. It takes time, effort, and perseverance. Just as you build and tone your body's muscles through exercise and weight training, you must exercise your intuitive and psychic muscles to strengthen them.

Most of us will use our psychic "superpowers" to benefit ourselves and our family and friends. Others will desire to become professional psychics and mediums. It can be a rewarding and fulfilling career. Again, it will take a great deal of training, practice, and dedication to the craft. You cannot (although some people do) simply read a book, take a course and immediately be open for business. That would be doing a great disservice to you, your clients, the psychic community, and, in the case of mediumship, the spirit world.

You may be drawn to the excitement and glamor depicted on television by psychic personalities such as Thomas John, James VanPraagh, or Teresa Caputo, and you want to be like them. Truth be told, even among professional psychics, few are destined to be on the world's stage. Be grateful for those who are. Those individuals have opened doors and paved the way for the rest of us. They also tend to take a lot of very public and harsh criticism and scrutiny along with their celebrity.

No matter how you choose to use your psychic gifts, the activities and exercises in this book will help you connect to and enhance your natural psychic abilities. Think of them as games to play. Explore your capabilities and have fun.

This guidebook is intended to be your companion on your journey of discovering and strengthening your unique psychic connections. Record your progress along the way in a journal or notebook. It will encourage you during times when you feel your learning isn't going as quickly or as smoothly as you'd like, or when it seems you're just not getting it. Plus, it will be fun to see how far you've traveled when you look back at where you've been.

To quote the prophet and Spiritualist, Andrew Jackson Davis, "Everything I've written I believe, at this time, to be true. My thoughts may change as I learn and discover more, and that is as it should be, but for now, this is what I know."

Onward to your psychic adventure!

INTUITION

"Cease trying to work everything out with your minds. It will get you nowhere. Live by intuition and inspiration and let your whole life be Revelation." -**Eileen Caddy**

EACH OF US IS BORN with intuition. It's that still small voice or inner knowing, a hunch or gut feeling we all experience at one time or another. It's sometimes dismissed as coincidence or a twist of fate. Intuition is our "Spirit (God) nudge," and if we allow it, intuition can help guide us in our day to day living.

Intuition is not the same as your conscience. Your conscience is your moral compass, an inner sense, or feeling that tells you if your behavior is morally right or wrong according to societal norms. Going against your conscience can leave you with feelings of guilt or shame, while going against your intuition can leave you shaking your head and thinking, "I should have listened."

For instance, you may ask your intuition if you should take a certain route to work or school or to an appointment, and it replies "no." You listen and travel a different way. You later discover that your intuition saved you from being stuck in a traffic jam which would have caused you to be an hour late. Or you heed the sudden urge to slow down while you're driving, only to have a deer leap out in front of you, one you would surely have hit had you not listened to your intuition.

Consider these incidents from the 9/11 terrorist attacks in 2001 involving the Twin Towers in New York City:

Holly Winter was to have attended a surprise breakfast with friends in one of the towers. Her mother decided to visit from out of town and insisted on meeting that day because "it felt like the right time to visit." Holly cancelled her plans with her friends. Her friends perished.

Actors Mark Wahlberg and Seth McFarlane were to have been on American Airlines Flight 11 (one of the planes that crashed into the Twin Towers), but Wahlberg changed his mind at the last minute, chartering a plane instead. McFarlane arrived at the airport too late to board.

Did intuition, coincidence, or a twist of fate spare these individuals and numerous others? I believe so.

Your intuition is accessible to you 24/7, wants only the highest and greatest good for you, and will only speak the truth.

Your exchange with intuition will typically be very brief, perhaps a fleeting feeling or just a few words, primarily yes or no. I usually hear a word or two in my psychic ear, when my intuition speaks to me, and feel a slight twinge or quickening in my solar plexus at the same time; as if the two were connected by an invisible wire.

Intuition can be very persistent. For example, you may be nudged to get a physical, yet you keep putting it off. However, when you finally have the exam, a medical issue you were unaware of is discovered.

While intuition may guide you to zig instead of zag, you get to choose whether to adhere to the message or not because you have free will. It will not judge or criticize you for your choices.

Additionally, you will need to discern intuition's warning signal from your own fear. For instance, I am afraid of flying. Whenever I'm about to board the plane, everything within me screams "NO," but that is my fear, not my intuition saying I shouldn't fly.

An easy way to become familiar with your intuition is to ask it simple yes or no questions. Ask it about everything, no matter how insignificant it may seem. It's good practice. Pay attention to where you *feel, hear,* or *sense* intuition's answer in or on your body. As earlier mentioned, I usually hear intuition's response in my psychic ear and get a twinge in my gut.

Examples of questions you might ask your intuition are:

- Should I wear this blouse/suit/outfit today?
- Is it going to rain? Do I need an umbrella?
- Is this a good time to go to the store? Library? Post office?
- Is this class (or <u>blank</u>) appropriate for me?
- Would (blank) be a good place for me to go on vacation?

Have you ever met someone you felt an immediate inexplicable connection with or someone you absolutely did not like for no apparent reason at all? You are picking up energetic impressions about them, and your intuition is giving you signals.

Asking your intuition for information about personal relationships can be somewhat tricky, and not because your intuition won't give you an accurate response. As human beings, we want what we want. We let our emotions (or hormones) get in the way, and often ignore our intuition's voice. Think of a past or perhaps a current relationship and see if this rings true for you. Trust your intuition.

When you ask a question of your intuition, pay attention to whether the answer is yes or no because you **want** the answer to be yes or no. Should this be the case, it is **YOU** answering the question, not your intuition.

What happens if you've asked your intuition a question, and the answer you receive seems incorrect? Consider that you may not have heard the answer correctly, or that you may have missed your intuition's signal. Perhaps you second-guessed yourself. Maybe it wasn't your intuition that answered, but your subconscious mind instead. Keep practicing!

Another way to get a response from your intuition is to say, "I need the truth of the situation shown to me," and then listen for its reply. Remember - intuition will answer quickly and without hesitation.

My husband and I have a nearly nightly ritual of playing the card game, *Cribbage*. When I look at my cards and am not clear which cards I should play, I ask my intuition for help. When I listen to my intuition, it's always correct. It's a fun game for me to play within the game, and I love being delighted by the accuracy of my intuition. My husband is aware that I do this because I've told him I do. He just shakes his head. I never ask what cards HE is playing. I only ask what cards would be best for ME to play.

The next time you play a game and are unclear what move to make, try asking your intuition to guide you. In fact, ANY time a move in your life isn't clear, ask its guidance.

One morning I went to the post office. Only two service windows were open, and there were about six people already in line. What a perfect time to play with my intuition.

I asked whether the male or female postal clerk would help me. I clearly heard "**female**."

As the line moved forward, it became obvious the male clerk would be assisting me, and that my intuition had been wrong. I was confused and disappointed in myself. I obviously was not as tuned in as I thought I was.

When it was my turn, I approached the service window. I told the clerk what I needed help with. He replied he hadn't trained for that yet and would I please go to the next window so **SHE** could help me. Intuition for the win!

I have a business creating beaded art for the home and garden, which I call Glitter Chains. I have literally thousands of beads all neatly separated and stored in a multi-drawered organizer, one typically used to contain hardware such as nuts, bolts, and screws.

One day, I was working on a Glitter Chain project in my living room. The beads, my other supplies, and the project were sitting on a small table, so I would have easy access to the materials I needed.

After working on my project for a couple of hours, I had to stop and leave the house for a short time. I didn't want to go through the hassle of moving my supplies or the project because I knew I would be returning home in less than an hour, so I decided to let everything be. As I got up to leave the house, I clearly heard "**BEADS.**" I knew my intuition meant I should move the beads, but I didn't want to. The organizer is heavy, I was right in the middle of my project, and it would be inconvenient to put everything away, go run my errand, come back home, and get resettled.

I left things as they were and went to run my errand. I don't know if the cat or dog knocked into the table while I was gone, but when I came back an hour later, the bead organizer was lying on the floor along with my project, with thousands of beads scattered across the PATTERNED carpet! It took me ten times longer to pick up those beads and put them back in their proper order than it would have taken to do as intuition had guided me to do in the first place.

"**Keys,**" my intuition said just as I was about to walk out the back door, arms full of packages. "I have my keys in my pocket," I confidently assured myself.

"**Keys,**" my intuition said again. "In my pocket, I'm sure of it."

"**KEYS,**" my intuition said for a third time, only slightly louder and with a noticeable nudge. (I can be just a tad stubborn.) I put my packages down and reached into my pocket. There were no keys! They were on the kitchen counter. I'd neglected to pick them up when I grabbed my phone. I was so glad I listened to my intuition. It was mid-winter in Ohio and my husband was out of town for the day. I would have been locked out of my house until his return.

How many times have you said, "I **KNEW** I should have done this instead of that" or "I **KNEW** I should have listened to myself?" Your intuition always has your best interest in mind. As you learn to recognize its subtle voice and signals and gain confidence in its guidance, you will come to rely on it more and more.

Psychic/medium Echo Bodine (www.echobodine.com) lives her life completely by intuition, asking it about EVERYTHING - when to pay bills, go to the store, work in the garden, make a call or offer a class, and even when to accept a teaching engagement. She has several videos on YouTube about intuition. They are insightful and full of good information. I encourage you to watch them.

INTUITION VS PSYCHIC ABILITY

Are intuition and psychic ability the same? There are those who would disagree, but for me, the answer is yes, and no. Let me explain.

While intuition and psychic ability are often used interchangeably and are essentially the same, I consider them to be like two separate branches of one tree. They are linked together because they come from the same primary energy source, yet each branch is individual.

Although intuition and psychic ability come from the same energy source, I differentiate the two in this way: Intuition is psychic energy used to guide **you** personally - your personal psychic connection with Source. Psychic ability is psychic energy to be used for the benefit of **others**.

THOUGHTS FOR CONSIDERATION:

- Become best friends with your intuition. Learn to recognize its voice and trust what it tells you. Your intuition will never lead you astray.

- How does YOUR intuition speak to you? What intuitive signals do you receive and how do you receive them? What does your intuition sound like? How does it feel?
- Has your intuition ever seemed to have been wrong? How did you know it was your intuition and not your conscious/subconscious mind?
- Journal about times when you listened to your intuition and had surprising results. How has listening to your intuition served you? Have there been times you ignored or resisted listening to your intuition?
- What are ways in which you've used your intuition?
- Maybe you've felt your intuitive messages were just coincidences. Keep a separate "coincidence" journal. It will help boost your confidence by showing you how often you naturally received intuitive and psychic impressions and how accurate those impressions were.

EMPATHS

"You do not have to continuously monitor all the disaster in the world. You are not in charge of outrage and grief. Witness it. Feel the feeling. Take action. But remember, love is where you live."
—Nanea Hoffman

AN EMPATH IS ONE WHO can sense or feel another's emotional or physical energy. This applies to the energy of locations as well. While being empathic can be a useful aid when doing psychic work, you do not want to have your energy depleted or entangled with someone else's.

There are those empathic individuals who are extremely sensitive to the energies around them. For them, being out in the world can be difficult and exhausting. Going shopping at the mall can leave them feeling drained. Even being at a party with people they enjoy can be energetically depleting. These highly sensitive persons must work extra hard at grounding and centering themselves and staying that way.

We live in this world, so we need to be able to navigate through it and to function in it. None of us are meant to be victims to our gifts, nor should we be held hostage by them.

No matter your level of sensitivity, you must set boundaries for yourself, practice self-care, and tend to your spiritual hygiene. Cleanse and protect your auric field at least once daily, but however often is necessary, using the method of your choice. It needn't be a lengthy process. Here are simple things you can do to cleanse your energy field:

- Clap your hands or flick your fingertips.
- Ring a bell or chime and imagine the sound dispersing negativity.
- Brush stagnant energy down your arms and away from you.

Water is a perfect cleanser. Whenever you wash your hands or shower, imagine excess psychic debris going down the drain. Additionally, you can spritz a mixture of water and an essential oil over yourself. Aligning your chakras (as in Chakra Exercise #1) or smudging may also be beneficial. If you choose to smudge, be mindful not to use vulnerable or endangered plant materials.

I believe we are always Divinely protected. There are ways, however, to add extra layers of protection, should you feel you need to.

- Wear or place in your pocket a crystal or gemstone.
- Burn a special candle.
- Say a prayer or mantra that has significance for you.
- Wear a mirror necklace to deflect negative energy or the energy of another individual. You can make one for yourself or purchase one at www.HolisticArts.net.
- Place a piece of metal foil tape or a mirror in your pocket or bra, reflective side facing outward, away from your body.
- Drape a scarf around the back of your neck or apply a drop of an essential oil to the occipital ridge, the place at the back of your neck where your skull meets your spine, to ward off negativity and prevent "psychic" attacks from energy vampires.

THOUGHTS FOR CONSIDERATION:

- In what ways do you practice self-care?
- How would you practice self-care or assist others with self-care in the following scenarios?
  - Tense familial relationships
  - Work situations involving a demanding boss or difficult co-workers
  - Troublesome neighbors
  - Needy clients or friends

Psychic Gifts:
Getting to Know Your "Clairs"

YOUR PSYCHIC SENSES are known as "clairs," meaning clear. You typically have one or two psychic senses that are more dominant, although you may use the others from time to time.

The psychic senses are as follows:

Clairvoyance – clear seeing

Claircognizance – clear knowing

Clairaudience – clear hearing

Clairsentience – clear feeling & Clairempathy – clear (emotional) feeling

Clairtangency – clear touch

Clairgustance – clear tasting

Clairsalience – clear smelling

Pay attention to where both on and in your physical body you receive your psychic "hits" or signals. These may be goosebumps, pain, or a change in temperature among other things. This is very important. It's your unique psychic language and will help you to discern true psychic messages from internal/external chatter and interference.

The following exercises will help you identify your dominant psychic sense(s) and what you have a natural affinity for.

With your eyes open, think about your kitchen. Can you envision the countertop? The sink? Do you see where your coffee pot, canisters, and paper towel are? You'll even see the dirty dishes in the sink if you have any! You aren't remembering where they are, you are *seeing* them in your mind's eye. Notice on your physical body the place you are viewing your kitchen. That location is most likely between and slightly above your physical eyes. This area is known as your third or psychic eye. Did you notice the image of your kitchen came to you instantly? You didn't even have to think about it.

Imagine yourself at a lake or ocean on a breezy sunny day. Can you hear the waves as they come to shore or the squawk of seagulls flying overhead? Can you notice the sound of children playing in the sand? Where you *hear* those sounds is where your psychic hearing takes place.

What images come to your mind when you think of yellow? Is it the sun, a school bus, or a banana? Do you *see* a flash of color? What sensations do you get when you think of yellow? Is there a *feel* to it? A warmth? A density? Does it vibrate or pulsate?

Our most powerful physical sense is the sense of smell, and often, our deceased loved ones will impress a scent on us to let us know they are near. See if your psychic nose can "remember" the smell of these scents: the aroma of a rose or your favorite flower, fresh cut grass, your grandfather's aftershave or grandmother's perfume, pipe tobacco or campfire. Were the memory of these odors brief or did they linger?

Here are two additional scenarios to consider:

When you think of going to a carnival or county fair, what attracts you most? What are you drawn to? Can you see (clairvoyance) the bright flashing lights and the rides? Are you able to hear (clairaudience) the sounds of the carnival music or the noises of the animals in the barn exhibits? Maybe your mouth waters at the memory of the taste (clairgustance) or smell (clairsalience) of your favorite fair food. Do you feel (clairsentience) a sense of excitement in the air?

Allow the image of a lemon to come forward in your mind's eye and note its shape and color. Imagine holding the lemon in your hand. Can you feel the texture of its skin, the dimples of its surface? Does it feel cool or warm? Imagine slicing the lemon in half. Can you hear the knife slicing through the layers of the fruit? Can you smell its aroma? Notice how the fruit glistens. See the lemon seeds inside. Bring the lemon to your lips, anticipating its flavor on your tongue. Take a bite of the lemon. Can you taste it?

In each of the two examples just given, what did you find easier? Visualizing the fair and lemon? Hearing sounds or smelling aromas? Experiencing taste or flavor? As mentioned before, these are clues to your most developed psychic senses. We all have at least one or two that are dominant, but we have the capability and capacity to use all of them. It just takes practice.

THOUGHTS FOR CONSIDERATION:
- Which psychic senses are currently your strongest?
- Which senses would you like to develop?

ENERGY

We are slowed down sound and light waves, a walking bundle of frequencies tuned into the cosmos. We are souls dressed up in sacred biochemical garments and our bodies are the instruments through which our souls play their music."

-Albert Einstein

EVERYTHING IN THE UNIVERSE is made up of energy; from people, animals, and plants, to buildings, machinery, and all the materials needed to create something physical. Energy isn't limited only to the people, places, and things we can see and observe. Air, wind, sound, thoughts, words, and actions all have energy as well. When you gather psychic impressions, you are reading energy.

Some people can see or feel energetic fields (auras) surrounding living beings or objects, but what about the energy of the things you can't see? Consider times when you've been listening to music and you got goosebumps on your arms or legs or a shiver up your spine. You were feeling the song's energetic vibrations, even if you couldn't see them. In addition to those goosebumps or chills, you may see the hairs on your arms raise or experience tingling on your scalp. These are all physical indications you are feeling and reacting to energy.

The body is a highly sensitive, finely tuned machine. You can feel a single strand of hair run across your face or the sharp pain of a nearly invisible sliver in your finger, making your body an excellent instrument for reading and registering energy.

The energy centers within the body are constantly projecting and receiving energetic information. The human hand alone has an average of 17,000 touch receptors and nerve endings located in the palms, making the palms of the hand, along with your fingers (the index finger being the most sensitive) incredibly adept at detecting pressure, temperature, and textures, along with variations of each. Why is this important? When you are scanning or feeling for energy, your hand and fingers make perfect tools to detect subtle energetic nuances and variants!

ENERGY FIELD GAMES

The following activities are meant to assist you in learning to feel energy and notice its subtle differences.

ENERGY FIELD EXERCISE #1

Position your hands in front of you, palms facing each other about an inch apart. What do you notice about the space between your hands? Is there a coolness or warmth? Is there a feeling of density? A tingling sensation? Nothing at all? The energetic information you receive may take a moment to process. Be patient.

ENERGY FIELD EXERCISE #2

Activate the energy centers in your hands (palm energy centers) by briskly rubbing your hands together either back and forth or in a circular motion for a few seconds. It will also heighten the feeling of energy felt in your hands and signals to the Universe that you are ready to receive information and/or project energy.

Next, place your hands in front of you, an inch or so apart, palms facing each other as you did in the previous exercise. What does the energy between your palms feel like? Do you notice a difference from the first exercise?

The difference between exercises #1 and #2 may be subtle or quite noticeable. In both cases, you are feeling your energy field, but I think you will find that rubbing your hands together activates the energy centers in your palms much quicker and heightens their sensitivity.

How far can you separate your hands before you no longer feel the energy between them?

ENERGY FIELD EXERCISE #3

Activate the energy centers in your hands.

Bring your hands approximately an inch from your face, palms toward you. Do you notice anything different about the energy emanating from your hands now than you did in the previous exercises?

ENERGY FIELD EXERCISE #4

In this exercise, you will learn how to create an energy ball.

Briskly rub the palms of your hands together for a few seconds.

Cupping your hands together, imagine holding a ball. Is there a feeling of warmth or other temperature to it? Do you detect a weight to the ball? Whatever you notice is perfectly fine. How would you describe this energy? How long are you able to hold this energy in your hands?

When you are finished, shake your hands to dispel any energy that may be lingering there. Do this after each exercise.

ENERGY FIELD EXERCISE #5

Create an energy ball and cup your hands together.

While still holding the ball, slowly separate your hands about an inch or two apart. What do you notice? Is there a coolness or warmth between them? Is there a density? Do you notice a pulsating or tingling sensation? Is there anything else about this energy you sense? How does this differ, if at all, from exercise #4?

Continue separating your hands. At what point are you unable to feel or sense the energy of the ball?

ENERGY FIELD EXERCISE #6

Try doing the previous exercises with your eyes closed. What are your observations? Do you notice any difference in the feel of the energy with your eyes open as opposed to them being closed? Which way did you like best?

ENERGY FIELD EXERCISE #7

Activate the energy centers in your palms.

Open one hand with its palm up. With the index finger of the opposite hand and without touching your finger to your open palm, draw a circle into your palm. Feel the energy flowing in the circle. Can you slow the energy down? Speed it up? Can you change its direction? Can you change the temperature of the energy? Is there anything else you notice?

ENERGY FIELD EXERCISE #8

Take a standing position and activate your palm energy centers.

As you feel the energy emanating from your hands, slowly run your hands over your body, keeping them an inch or two above your body, scanning your body's energy field. Scan over your entire head, torso, arms, and legs. Become aware of any dense or thin feeling energy, any cool or hot spots, or places where your energy field may seem stagnant or pulsating.

Try this same exercise from a sitting position and then from a prone position. Does one position make it easier for you to feel the energy than another? What, if any, differences did you observe between the three?

As you do these activities, realize how much more than a physical body you are - you are a vibrant bundle of energy!

You will need a partner or partners for the remainder of these energy field exercises.

ENERGY FIELD EXERCISE #9

Choose one person to create an energy ball and practice passing it back and forth. Notice if and how the energy ball changes with each passing.

If you are with more than one person, switch who creates the energy ball within the group and see if that changes anything.

ENERGY FIELD EXERCISE #10

Everyone in the group creates an individual energy ball.

If there are only two of you, pass the balls back and forth, adding an additional ball each time you receive it.

GAMES PSYCHICS PLAY | 31

If there are more than two of you, let one person begin by passing their energy ball to the person next to them. When the ball comes to you, add yours to it. Feel the expansion of the energy as it is passed between you.

How large an energy ball can you create? Is it lighter or heavier? Does the feeling of the energy change? Is there a point at which you can no longer hold the energy ball?

ENERGY FIELD EXERCISE #11

Choose a "working" partner, while the other partner sits or stands.

Working partner: activate your hand's energy centers. Placing your hands an inch or two above your partner's body, slowly scan their energy field. What do you notice about the energy surrounding their body?

For example, you may find the energy in the area around your partner's throat feels different than the rest of their body. Maybe the density or temperature in that area feels different from other areas. Describe what you notice. Perhaps **YOU** get a sensation of wanting to scream or clear your **OWN** throat when you are near the throat of your partner. You may even hear words like "stuck" or "pain" to describe your partner's throat or see a psychic image like red flames. Try to convey what you are receiving energetically without defining or interpreting what it is.

Let your partner affirm or invalidate your findings. For instance: if you say to your partner, "the area around your left ankle feels hot," but your partner says their ankle is fine, don't be discouraged. Trust what you are feeling. It's quite possible you are picking up energy from an old injury they've forgotten about, or a psychic impression about something that will occur. Simply relay the information you receive to your partner.

As you develop and gain confidence in your skills, you may notice the energy arrives more quickly or more strongly.

We all make judgements from time to time about others based on their appearances, whether that be their gender, age, ethnicity, body size, choice of dress, way of speaking, or any number of other observances. Do you notice any of these making a difference in your readings? Practicing and doing energetic work will cause you to examine your own personal biases. Be fearless in doing so.

(This illustration is simply meant to distinguish the various auric layers and energy centers, not to imply their colors or sizes.)

Auras and Chakras

EVERYTHING, WHETHER LIVING or inanimate, is made of energy, with their molecules moving at different speeds. For instance, the molecules of a table will move much more slowly than those of a living human being.

We are naturally able to sense energy. You can tell when a room is sizzling with excitement or heavy with sadness. In each case, you are feeling the energy fields not only of the individuals in the room, but of the room itself and the energy it has absorbed.

The human energy field is made up of the auric field, which encases the physical body and the chakras - energy centers located within and around the body. Whether you are an energy worker, healer, psychic, or medium, a basic knowledge of this energy system can enhance your work.

AURAS

You may recognize the auric field as a thin outline surrounding a body or object. Did you know that some believe the halos depicted in paintings and drawings of holy men and women are auras? We typically lose the ability to see auras around the age of seven or eight, most likely because we don't hear anyone else talking about auras or we are told to quit talking about them or that they don't exist. Consider a baby not making eye contact with you, instead seeming to look at something around your head, or a toddler excitedly telling you about something while their eyes dart all around you. Could they be witnessing a fantastic color display put on by your auric field?

When my youngest son was about five or six, he would talk about all the colors he could see surrounding me. Sadly, he quit discussing auras and colors by the time he was eight, even though I encouraged him to continue. He now says he doesn't remember ever doing such a thing.

With practice, you can regain the ability to see auras. It's a matter of retraining the rods and cones in your eyes. These next exercises will help you.

AURA GAMES
AURA EXERCISE #1
When trying to view auras, relax your eyes and look at your subject with a soft gaze, not a hard stare. Here's how:

Look straight ahead and without moving your head or eyes, view your surroundings peripherally. Notice how you must soften your gaze to do so? This is the look or softening you will need to help you see auras. You can also try looking just below or beyond an object, as this too, will help you soften your gaze.

AURA EXERCISE #2

Do you remember the *Magic Eye* 3D picture books that were popular in the 1990's? Practice viewing the pictures they contain. The purpose of practicing with these pictures is to help train your eyes to look beyond what you directly see. You can find books with these images at your local bookstore or online.

AURA EXERCISE #3

Place your hand on a sheet of plain white paper. Relax your eyes and soften your gaze while looking at the space between YOU and your hand. Lowering your eyelids slightly may help, too. Can you see an outline around your hand? Is there a color to it?

Try using a sheet of color paper. Try a variety of colors. What are your observations? Is it easier for you to view the aura against certain colors? Does the color or width of the aura change depending on the background color?

AURA EXERCISE #4

Do exercise #3 using your foot. Do the auras of your hand and foot appear different?

AURA EXERCISE #5

Practice viewing auras in various types of lighting such as candlelight, fluorescent, outdoors, etc.

Aura Exercise #6
Try viewing the aura of a pet, tree, or house plant.

AURA EXERCISE #7

A partner will be needed for this exercise. Ask your partner to stand against a light-colored wall so you can view their aura. Once you're able to see it, ask your partner to move their arm slowly above their head. Can you follow their auras' movement?

AURA EXERCISE #8

After you've learned to see the aura, begin noticing places on your subject where the aura appears to be wider or narrower, duller, or brighter. Are you able to see color? What else do you notice?

THOUGHTS FOR CONSIDERATION:

• Many psychic fairs and expos have individuals who will take a photograph of your aura. It might be interesting for you to have one done and interpreted. Don't rely solely on the photographer's interpretation; what do YOU see?

CHAKRAS

As a practicing foot reflexologist, I often found energetic disturbances at reflex points. For instance, when working on the foot, I might notice what feels like a disruption of energy at the heart reflex. Knowing the heart was located within the heart chakra area, I could then feel (read) if this were caused by something on a physical, emotional, mental, or spiritual level. Being able to determine one level from another came after much practice and observation. Having a basic understanding of the human energy system and its chakras helped me to be a more effective practitioner.

Chakras are spinning energy centers within the body. Each chakra has equal importance to your energetic health, and one chakra should not be valued above another. Chakras process subtle energy, converting it into chemical, hormonal, and cellular changes within the body.

We have a physical heart but that is not the heart chakra. We have a third eye chakra, yet we don't have three physical eyes. While there are no actual physical chakras, these energy centers can affect us physically, emotionally, mentally, or spiritually. Because there are no physical chakras, it is extremely important that you practice feeling not only the energy around you, but that of the specific chakra energy centers.

What follows is a basic guide to the eight main chakras found within the human energy system, with a few ways to support or boost them including the use of essential oils. By no means is this a comprehensive list. They are only suggestions. Use your intuition to determine what is right for you.

Should you choose to incorporate the use of essential oils into your practice, be sure they are pure and not synthetic, as synthetic oils have no healing properties. For your safety, always use essential oils with a carrier oil such as coconut or almond oil. I personally prefer Amrita Aromatherapy's line of essential oils.

ROOT CHAKRA

The root chakra is located at the base of the abdomen. It is associated with survival; our basic need to be fed, nurtured, sheltered, and to procreate. Fear is also connected with the root chakra, which activates our "fight or flight" response when our sense of survival is threatened.

Aligned: feel grounded/secure, all basic needs (food/shelter/ money/sex) being met, self-confident

Misaligned: fear, anger/aggression, feels victimized, overindulges in physical and material aspects of life, obsesses about money, mistrustful of others, fear of lack, hoarding

Affects: feet, legs, digestive system, emotional imbalances

WAYS TO SUPPORT AND BOOST
THE ROOT CHAKRA:

Color: red

Food: raspberries, strawberries, cherries, red apples, cranberries, tomatoes, root vegetables such as sweet potatoes, beets, and parsnips, kidney beans, red meat

Essential Oils: frankincense, sandalwood, patchouli, vetiver

Gemstones: ruby, hematite, black obsidian, tourmaline, jasper, smoky quartz

Affirmations: I am safe. I have all I need.

SACRAL CHAKRA

The sacral chakra is located 1-2 inches below the navel and is associated with sexuality, sensuality, creativity, and our self-esteem. It is from this chakra that sexual feelings are expressed. Feelings of shame is often connected with this chakra.

Aligned: good body awareness, high self-love/self-esteem, lives creatively, has healthy regard and relationship with one's sexuality, gratitude for past experiences, deep joy, pursuit of passions

Misaligned: inability to express oneself sensually and creatively, inability to experience sexual pleasure, feelings of inadequacy reflected as possessiveness, jealousy, compulsive or obsessive sexual behavior, feeling victimized, picky, distracted, hopeless because of past experiences, depression, commitment issues, creativity blocks

Affects: sacral vertebrae, circulatory, urinary, and reproductive systems, depression

WAYS TO SUPPORT AND BOOST
THE SACRAL CHAKRA:

Color: orange

Food: oranges, mangos, cantaloupe, peaches, carrots, sweet potatoes, pumpkin, dark chocolate, salmon, nuts

Essential Oils: patchouli, neroli, orange, ylang-ylang

Gemstones: carnelian, alexandrite, coral, amber, topaz

Affirmations: I am a channel of creativity. I am free to be myself.

Solar Plexus Chakra

The solar plexus chakra (also known as the seat of the soul) is located 1-2 inches above the navel and is associated with the assimilation of emotions, and personal power. Feelings of anger are often connected with this chakra.

Aligned: centered, high self-esteem, confident, self-control, ability to manifest material abundance, feels good interacting with environment, freedom to explore, generous, open

Misaligned: overblown ego to mask insecurity with outer world, withdrawn, bottled up emotions, excess, unmotivated, emotional eating, feelings of panic and worry, fear, mistrust, fear of victimization

Affects: spleen, liver, pancreas, and stomach including stomach pains, chronic indigestion, ulcers

WAYS TO SUPPORT AND BOOST
THE SOLAR PLEXUS CHAKRA:

Color: yellow

Food: bananas, lemon, pineapple, corn, ginger, honey, complex carbohydrates, and whole grain

Essential Oils: pine, bergamot, vanilla, peppermint, chamomile

Gemstones: citrine, amber, tiger's eye

Affirmations: I am confident in my ability. I am strong and balanced.

HEART CHAKRA

The heart chakra is located at the area around the heart, and is associated with self-love and unconditional love, NOT romantic love. It acts as the bridge between the lower three physical chakras (root, sacral, and solar plexus), and the three upper chakras (throat, third eye, crown).

Aligned: self-care, loving and supportive relationships, ability to forgive, feels honor, respect, and deep love for life, optimism, joy, compassion, love for self and others

Misaligned: gossiping, unhappiness with self, self-pity, feels attacked, burdened, hypersensitive, negativity, pessimism, feelings of unworthiness, paranoia

Affects: heart, lungs, upper torso, shoulders, arms, and hands, low energy, poor digestion

WAYS TO SUPPORT AND BOOST THE HEART CHAKRA:

Color: green or pink

Food: raw green vegetables such as broccoli, brussel sprouts, kale, spinach, lettuce, and cucumbers, avocado, lime, kiwi, green apples, olive oil

Essential Oils: rose, geranium, ylang-ylang, basil, eucalyptus, jasmine

Gemstones: rose quartz, pink or green tourmaline, green jade, emerald

Affirmations: I am enough. I am love.

THYMUS CHAKRA

The thymus chakra is located between the heart and throat

chakras. It is associated with our physical thymus, which regulates our autoimmune system. This chakra assists with transitions, and in balancing and uniting the throat and heart chakras - the physical with the spiritual.

Aligned: energetic, motivated, seeks connection and expression of the Divine, willingness to forgive and show compassion

Misaligned: depressed, unmotivated, spiritual bypassing to avoid difficult issues in life

Affects: lymphatic system

WAYS TO SUPPORT AND BOOST THE THYMUS CHAKRA:

Color: teal/aquamarine

Food: broccoli, lettuce, mustard greens, kale

Essential Oils: thyme, eucalyptus, clary sage, lavender

Gemstones: turquoise, aquamarine, amazonite

Affirmation: I am strong, healthy, and powerful.

THROAT CHAKRA

The throat chakra is located at the throat and is associated with the power of expression. A blockage in the throat chakra will often appear as an inability to clearly speak or voice one's thoughts and feelings.

Aligned: speak from a place of knowing and deep inner truth, self-confidence, integrity, honesty, lucid dreaming

Misaligned: inability to express one's feelings and thoughts or communicate well, lying, dishonesty, gossiping, denial, feel unheard, aloneness

Affects: neck, throat, jaw, teeth, thyroid, sinuses, swollen glands, neck/shoulder pain

WAYS TO SUPPORT AND BOOST THE THROAT CHAKRA:

Color: blue

Food: blueberries, blackberries, elderberries, plums, raw honey, herbal teas, water, watery foods, yogurt, seaweed

Essential Oils: lavender, cypress, sage, mint, blue chamomile, tea tree

Gemstones: lapis lazuli, blue lace agate, larimar, celestite, turquoise

Affirmation: I speak the truth clearly.

Third Eye Chakra

The third eye chakra is located at the forehead between the brows. It is associated with intuition, insight, inspiration, our psychic connection with others, and the ability to see clearly.

Aligned: open to new ideas, seeks answers from Source, inspired by Higher Source, sense of purpose, desire to grow and learn

Misaligned: closed minded, mind wanders, unable to focus, lack of direction or purpose

Affects: ears, eyes, sinuses, coordination and balance, sleep disturbances, tension headaches

WAYS TO SUPPORT OR BOOST THE THIRD EYE CHAKRA:

Color: indigo

Food: purple grapes, eggplant, boysenberries, purple cabbage, eggs, cacao, "brain" foods, chamomile tea

Essential Oils: cedarwood, eucalyptus, sandalwood, rosemary

Gemstones: amethyst, fluorite, moonstone, kyanite

Affirmations: I see clearly. I trust my intuition.

CROWN CHAKRA

The crown chakra is located just above the crown of the head, connecting us with our Higher Self.

Aligned: open, feels guidance from Higher Power, a sense of oneness, self-realization; seeking wisdom, joy, understanding

Misaligned: delusional, mood swings, confusion, disconnection, feelings of insignificance

Affects: central nervous system (CNS), headaches, depression, sensitivity to light

WAYS TO SUPPORT AND BOOST THE CROWN CHAKRA:

Color: violet or white

Food: mushrooms, garlic, ginger, coconut, lychee, onion, and fasting

Essential Oils: helichrysum, frankincense, myrrh, sage, lavender, juniper

Gemstones: quartz, howlite

Affirmations: I am One with all creation. I am One with the Universe.

CHAKRA ALIGNING GAMES
CHAKRA EXERCISE #1

While quietly sitting or lying down, perhaps even before you get out of bed in the morning, take a few deep, calming breaths. Starting at the root chakra, say to yourself or out loud, "My root chakra is open and balanced" or something along those lines. Move up to the sacral chakra, repeat, and so on throughout the entire chakra system. You may also wish to visualize each chakra's corresponding color as you state your mantra.

CHAKRA EXERCISE #2

Activate your palm energy centers.

Gently place your hands on or slightly above the location of your chakra centers. What do you observe? Do your chakras feel vibrant or sluggish? Is there a warmth or coolness and if so, to what degree? Do you notice a density associated with them? Can you sense calmness or chaos within the chakra energy centers? Is it possible that there is something affecting you on an emotional, physical, mental, or spiritual level that might cause that chakra to feel that way?

CHAKRA EXERCISE #3

You can do this exercise on your own or with others. Toning the Om mantra is a fun way to align and energize your chakras. This is not an exercise in how perfect your voice is or how well you sing. One of the most beautiful things I've ever heard was the sound of twenty-five individuals all chanting the Om mantra into their chakra energy centers. It sounded like a celestial choir!

The Om mantra contains 4 syllables: A-U-M and a silent syllable.

According to Yoga Culture in a blog dated November 5, 2017, "when pronounced correctly, Om actually sounds like aummm."

1. The first syllable is A and is pronounced like "awe."

2. The second syllable is U and is pronounced "ooo."

3. The third syllable is M and is pronounced like a long "mmm."

4. The fourth syllable is silent and begins when the sound from the third syllable fades into silence.

Begin toning the Om into your root chakra, experimenting with various pitches or tones until you feel its vibration within that center. Once you have the proper tone to energize your root chakra, repeat three times, holding the tone for approximately ten seconds each time.

Move up to the sacral chakra. Notice the toning vibration here.

Continue up the chakra system until you've completed toning Om into each energy center. Enjoy the sensation of having your entire chakra system energized!

CHAKRA EXERCISE #4

A partner is needed for this exercise.

Activate your palm energy centers. Placing your hands slightly above your partner's body, go over each chakra. What impressions are you getting? Be sure to notice any sensations in or on your **own** body as you are assessing your partner's chakra energy centers. For instance, while you are at your partner's heart chakra, you may get a heavy sensation in your chest. Could your partner be suffering from allergies that cause upper respiratory issues? Are you feeling an emotion? Perhaps your partner is experiencing some emotional heartache or euphoria, or something is weighing heavy on their heart. The more you practice using your own intuitive and psychic abilities in reading energy, the more accurate you will become.

CHAKRA EXERCISE #5*

As you proceed through this meditation, note the tone and resonance of each chakra. What is its hue or shade? Is it dull or vibrant? Where within each do you perceive scarring, tears, rips, or leakage? What is the energetic feel of each one and the system overall? What messages, if any, do your chakras have for you?

CHAKRA HEALING MEDITATION

Become comfortable, sitting up as straight as you can. Feel your feet flat on the surface below you. Relax your shoulders, pulling them down and back, opening your chest cavity.

After taking a few cleansing breaths in and out, allow your breathing to become relaxed and natural. If you wish, close your eyes.

Finding yourself fully supported in your seat, imagine your feet held firmly, yet gently, in place by the earth's magnetic pull. You may wish to feel as though there are roots sprouting from the bottoms of your feet, tethering you to the earth.

Gently bring your awareness to the area of your root chakra, located at the base of the spine. The root chakra is represented by the color red; its energy flows downward, anchored deeply into the earth. The root chakra is where you feel your basic primal needs are met: food, shelter, clothing, sex.

Notice the shade or tone of red the root chakra is presenting. Is its color vibrant or dull? Does the root chakra appear to be energetic or listless? What else do you notice? Do you feel grounded and secure, or do you feel victimized or mistrustful? Is there a space within the area of your root chakra that needs healing? Allow that recognition to come forward.

Feel the healing energy of Love filling the space of your root chakra energy center. You can feel safe, secure, firmly planted in the knowledge that you have everything you need; that you belong right here, right now.

See the red of the root chakra transmute into orange as the energy of the root chakra gently flows up to your sacral chakra, located in the area just below the navel. The sacral chakra is your creativity center and is where your inner child resides. Self-esteem, passion, deep joy, and sexual and sensual expression emanates from the sacral chakra.

Notice the shade or tone of orange the sacral chakra is presenting. Does its color seem to be vibrant and bright or dull and muted? What else do you notice? Are you able to express yourself in playful, creative ways or do you feel depressed or hopeless because of past experiences? Is there a space within the area of your sacral chakra that needs healing? Allow that recognition to come forward.

Feel the healing energy of Love filling the space of your sacral chakra energy center. You are a channel of creativity, free to express yourself and be fully who you are.

See the orange of the sacral chakra transmute into yellow as the energy of the sacral chakra gently flows up to your solar plexus chakra, located just above the navel. The solar plexus chakra is also known as the seat of the soul. It assimilates your emotions and personal power, your confidence and self-control.

Notice the shade or tone of yellow the solar plexus chakra is presenting. Does its color seem to sizzle with energy, or does it appear lethargic? What else do you notice? Do you feel confident and able to manifest abundance or do you bottle up your emotions and withdraw? Is there a space within the area of your solar plexus chakra that needs healing? Allow that recognition to come forward.

Feel the healing energy of Love filling the space of your solar plexus chakra energy center. You are strong and balanced and can be confident in your abilities.

See the yellow of the solar plexus chakra transmute into green or pink as the energy of the solar plexus chakra gently flows up to your heart chakra, located in the chest and the area of your physical heart. The heart chakra is associated with self-love and unconditional love and is not to be confused with romantic love. The heart chakra acts as a bridge between the lower three chakras and the upper three chakras.

Notice the shade or tone of green or pink the heart chakra is presenting. Does its color appear energetic or sluggish? What else do you notice? Do you find yourself with loving and supportive relationships, with love for yourself and others or do you engage in gossiping and bouts of self-pity or feelings of unworthiness? Is there a space within the area of your heart chakra that needs healing? Allow that recognition to come forward.

Feel the healing energy of Love filling the space of your heart chakra. You are enough. You are Love and you express Love in your words and actions.

See the green or pink of the heart chakra transmute into teal as the energy of the heart chakra gently flows up to your thymus chakra. This chakra is located at the space of your physical thymus, which is between the heart and throat chakras. The thymus chakra assists with transitions and in balancing and uniting the heart and throat, the physical with the spiritual. The thymus chakra is known as the spiritual heart and assists in opening you to your true essence.

Notice the shade or tone of teal the thymus chakra is presenting. Does its color appear to be vibrant or faded? What else do you notice? Do you find yourself feeling energetic and motivated, desiring connection with the Divine and to experience expression of the Divine, or do you feel unmotivated? Do you engage in spiritual bypassing, using spiritual lingo to avoid doing your emotional work? Is there a space within the area of your thymus chakra that needs healing? Allow that recognition to come forward.

Feel the healing energy of Love filling the space of your thymus chakra. You are strong, healthy, powerful.

See the teal of the thymus chakra transmute into blue as the energy of the thymus chakra gently flows up to your throat chakra. The throat chakra is located in the throat, and is your power of expression center, allowing you to voice your thoughts and feelings.

Notice the shade or tone of blue the throat chakra is presenting. Does its color appear vivid or washed out? What else do you notice? Are you able to speak clearly from a place of knowing and deep inner truth or do you find yourself unable to express your thoughts and feelings, engaging perhaps in passive aggressiveness or verbal bullying? Is there a space within the area of your throat chakra that needs healing? Allow that recognition to come forward.

Feel the healing energy of Love filling the space of your throat chakra. You speak the truth of your heart honestly and clearly.

See the blue of the throat chakra transmute into indigo as the energy of the throat chakra gently flows up to your third eye chakra, located on the forehead between the eyebrows. The third eye chakra is associated with intuition and insight, and your psychic connection with others.

Notice the shade or tone of indigo the third eye chakra is presenting. Does its color appear energetic or drab? What else do you notice? Do you find yourself open to new ideas, inspired by Higher Source or is your mind closed? Are you unable to focus? Is there a space within the area of your third eye chakra that needs healing? Allow that recognition to come forward.

Feel the healing energy of Love filling the space of your third eye chakra. You trust your intuition and psychic messages, your connection with the Divine.

See the indigo of the third eye chakra transmute into violet or white as the energy of the third eye chakra gently flows up to your crown chakra, located at the top of your head. The crown chakra connects you with your Higher Self and expands upward and outward.

Notice the shade or tone of violet or white the crown chakra is presenting. Does it appear bright and vibrant or dull and sluggish? What else do you notice? Do you feel or sense guidance from a Higher Power? Do you find yourself feeling a sense of Oneness to all that is, or do you feel flighty or disconnected? Is there a space within the area of your crown chakra that needs healing? Allow that recognition to come forward.

Feel the healing energy of Love filling the space of your crown chakra. You are One with all creation. You are One with the Universe.

In this space of peacefulness and calmness, take a moment to allow yourself to feel the integration of all the chakras within your energy field. Rest in the knowledge that you are a unique, one-of-a-kind, beautiful soul just waiting to express itself in the way that only you can. You are fully equipped to move forward.

When you are ready, gently bring your attention back to this time, this place, knowing healing has begun or taken place.

*You may record this guided meditation in your own voice to listen to. An audio version is available on my website to download: www.houseofthespirit.org.

GROUNDING, CLEARING,

AND PROTECTION

GROUNDING AND CLEARING yourself is imperative not only for your personal well-being, but to become an open, unobstructed psychic channel. Always do this before beginning any energy work and again afterward.

This can easily be done by intentionally taking in deep, cleansing breaths. Feel your feet firmly below you, supporting you. Silence your mind, calm your breath, still your body. A tranquil and relaxed state helps you receive messages clearly. Grounding and clearing yourself can be as simple as that.

Additional ways to ground yourself:

- Slow, deep breaths of fresh air
- Feel the sun on your skin
- Meditate
- Go out barefoot, feel your feet on the ground
- Massage your feet
- Work in the garden, dig in the dirt, touch plants

- Eat a piece of protein or chocolate
- Walk, run, jump, dance
- Sing
- Look at beautiful flowers, breathe in their fragrance
- Touch a tree, rock, or water
- Pet an animal
- Kiss

DO ANYTHING THAT PUTS YOU IN TOUCH WITH YOUR BODY!

QUICK AND EASY PROTECTION TECHNIQUES

Shower of Protection: While in the shower, imagine the spray of water washing away negativity and replacing it with a clear, protective glaze, sealing any cracks or holes in your aura.

Bubble: Imagine yourself wrapped in bubble wrap or surrounded by a large bubble. When you are traveling, surround your car, bus, train, airplane, etc. in it as well.

Angels and Spirit Guides: Ask your angels and spirit guides to stand beside you and protect you.

Energy of Spirit: Ask the energy of Spirit to fill your heart and flow throughout your body, and feel every cell of your being filled with the strength that this energy provides.

Spirit Animal: Imagine your spirit animal(s) at your side.

Tree: Feel yourself as strong as an oak tree. Ask the trees surrounding your home to act as sentinels to keep negativity away.

Prayer: Saying your favorite prayer is powerful. My personal favorite is the "Prayer of Protection," which can be found at the back of this book.

MEDITATION

A REGULAR MEDITATION practice will help advance your intuitive skills, psychic abilities, and mediumship, although it's not a requirement. Psychic growth may just take longer without it.

The mind can be a very noisy place and we can easily become distracted by our thoughts. Meditation helps to calm and still the mind. It helps you to master your conscious mind and move it out of the way. You can't have frenzied thoughts swirling around in your head and at the same time receive clear psychic signals. Does this mean you must sit still in silence for lengthy periods of time every day? No, not at all. You should, however, dedicate a portion of your day to just being still with as few distractions as possible. With practice, even those minor distractions will vanish. Perhaps you find five minutes in the morning just before or after you get out of bed is the perfect meditation time for you. Some find sitting in a chair or lying in bed to meditate works best for them. Either complete quiet or soft, gentle music playing in the background while meditating may be more conducive to stilling your mind. Experiment. Discover what is right for you. There is no one correct or best way to meditate.

Are you a beginner at meditation? Here are a few suggestions to get you started:

1. Choose the same time every day to meditate. Does 6 P.M. sound like a good time to meditate to you? Then meditate every day at 6 P.M., sitting in the same chair and same location. Begin meditating for only five minutes at a time, increasing the length of your meditation time as you can.

2. Clear your mind. Do not concern yourself about the events of the day during your meditation time. Imagine putting thoughts of those events into a jar and sealing it until meditation is over. Thoughts may wander back. Acknowledge them and set them aside.

3. Choose an image you like: a rose, a lake, or even a color. Maybe you have a favorite photo or painting you're drawn to. Perhaps there's a sound that is soothing to you such as a chime, birds chirping, or a water fountain. Whatever you choose, focus on it. Should your mind begin to wander, bring your focus back.

4. During meditation, close your eyes and look slightly upward into your third/psychic eye, which will activate it.

5. Breathe deeply and slowly.

A guided meditation may also be a good option. You can find meditations for calming your mind, healing your spirit, connecting with angels and spirit guides, or loved ones and so on.

Spending time in nature is another way to still and calm your mind. Sit outside and take a few minutes to feel the warmth of the sun on your face, or a gentle breeze blowing over you. Listen to the sounds of nature. Breath in the scents of your surroundings.

THOUGHTS FOR CONSIDERATION:

- Is meditation difficult for you? What makes it so? Rather than closing your eyes, you may find meditating with your eyes slightly open and with a softened gaze to work better for you.
- What might you do to make meditation easier?
- What are your favorite ways to meditate?
- What music do you like to use when you meditate?
- What songs pump you up and raise or elevate your energy level?
- If your energy is feeling frantic or scattered, what music calms you?

FOCUSING GAMES

As mentioned previously, being focused helps you to quiet the outside noise and inner mind chatter so you can concentrate on receiving psychic impressions and messages and distinguish them from your own thoughts. Here are exercises that can help you practice on focusing your mind.

FOCUS EXERCISE #1

Place a lit candle on a table or stand at eye level, approximately three feet away from you. Gaze softly at the candle flame for about a minute. Close your eyes. Hold onto the image of the candle flame in your mind and follow its afterimage for as long as you can. Should the afterimage fade away, gently bring it back to your mind's eye. Do this for as long as you can.

FOCUS EXERCISE #2

Rev. Janet Nohavec, in her book *Where Two Worlds Meet*, suggests closing your eyes and in your mind's eye, imagining a triangle. Make the triangle large and in any color you choose. Now place a circle within the triangle. Maintain that image for as long as you can. Repeat.

FOCUS EXERCISE #3

Go outdoors, find a comfortable spot, and close your eyes. Listen to all the sounds around you. What do you hear in your immediate surroundings? What do you hear in the distance?

Try to isolate just one sound and maintain focus on it for as long as you can, despite being aware of all the other sounds around you.

FOCUS EXERCISE #4
Listen to a song, focusing on the sound of just one instrument, the guitar for instance. See if you can hear and follow the sound of that instrument for the song's entirety. You could also choose the voice of a singer to follow.

Spirit Guides

AN ENTIRE SPIRITUAL TEAM is available to you at any time, day or night. Their purpose is to guide and protect you, offer you inspiration, encouragement, and comfort. They will not interfere with your life or decisions, and they will never judge or condemn you for your choices. They may shout out a warning, however, if you are in danger.

Your spiritual team consists of at least one main spirit guide who is assigned to you at birth. This guide will be with you up until you take your last breath, when you will be welcomed into the spirit world by family and loved ones who have gone before you. No one passes into the next world alone. Your spiritual team may also include angels and other etheric beings, ascended masters, family, friends, beloved pets, and animals. There may even be guides from other planets and galaxies on your team.

Situational guides and angels will offer temporary assistance. They are there for specific reasons such as pregnancy, job interviews, studying for exams, or even writing a book, and are gone once the event has occurred.

Your guides will often have the same interests as you because you speak the same language and have a shared commonality. For example, if you are an athlete, you probably have someone on your spiritual team who played that sport. Conversely, if you need help with your French studies, you most likely do not have a Latin professor assisting you.

There are many ways that your guides will make their presence known. Song lyrics might randomly pop into your head or you may regularly notice a certain sequence of numbers. Even a shift in energy can indicate their presence. Guidance is often provided through your dreams as you are more receptive when your mind isn't filled with the many to-dos of the day. Signs can take just about any form, and appear to you anytime, anywhere. You simply need to notice them.

I once asked my guide to show me a red rabbit to prove they were near. A few days went by with no sign of a red rabbit anywhere. While I was sitting at a stop light in a town I'd never been to, I glanced to my right, and there on a shop sign was the image of a red rabbit. Message received.

As I watched the Biden/Harris inauguration on TV, I said to my mom (who is in spirit) "well now, isn't this something." Within seconds of that thought, I got a Facebook notification on my phone. It was a post of Doris Day singing "Que Sera Sera," which was a phrase mom and I used to say to each other all the time. This told me she was there with me watching this historic event.

CONNECTING WITH YOUR SPIRIT GUIDES

How do you connect with your spirit guides or angels? Invite them in and ask for their assistance. No request is too large or too small, be it finding that perfect job or locating a parking spot. Your guides and angels are interested in all aspects of your life.

Try using the following imagery to connect with your spirit guides and angels to find out who they are. Be open to whomever may appear, the way they appear, and any messages you receive. (I once had a huge grizzly bear present itself as a guide, but I dismissed it. I'd been expecting someone with a human appearance!)

1. Ground and center yourself, allowing yourself to enter a relaxed meditative state with the intention of connecting with your spirit guide or angels.

2. Imagine yourself in a garden or outdoor sanctuary. Fill your garden with trees and plants and beautiful flowers of every color. Smell the fragrance of the earth. Feel a gentle breeze blow across your face. Feel the warmth of the sun. Hear the birds singing.

3. Find yourself sitting comfortably on a bench, a blanket, a log, or against a tree. Rest here for just a moment.

4. Notice a water fixture in your garden, perhaps a fountain, pond, or a small stream. See the water glisten in the sun, hear its movement.

5. Become aware of an entryway into your garden. Imagine a figure slowly coming toward you. Invite them to join you in this lovely space. This is your spirit guide.

6. Engage them in conversation. Ask them their name.

7. How will you recognize their presence in the future? Is there a sign or symbol they will use or a certain feeling you will have when they are near?

8. How would they like to be contacted?

9. What message(s) do they have for you?

10. Express your gratitude for them in your life and bid them goodbye.

PSYCHICS

"Every man has within himself latent faculties, undeveloped senses, by means of which the unseen world can be directly cognized, and to anyone who will take the trouble to evolve these powers, the whole world beyond the grave will lie open as the day."
–C. W. Leadbeater ("The Life After Death: And How Theosophy Unveils It")

ARE THERE CHARLATANS in the psychic field? Are there psychics who take advantage and prey on the vulnerable? Yes, of course there are, just as there are unsavory individuals in any profession. However, that unfortunate truth should not automatically negate all psychics or mediums. Most of the psychics and mediums I know are honest, everyday people who want to use their gifts and abilities to offer help and assistance to others.

Along your psychic travels, you'll encounter individuals all too ready and anxious to discredit you, refusing any notion that psychic and mediumship abilities exist. More than likely these individuals:

1. Don't recognize or acknowledge coincidences as psychic occurrences. For instance, knowing who's calling on the phone without looking at the caller ID or thinking of someone out of the blue and then hearing from them within a day or two.

2. Take the word of the church or other "experts" that such abilities are evil, unholy, or unnatural.

3. Have never tried to prove, but only disprove such abilities, and place validation only in what can be scientifically tested or physically seen.

Future events a psychic may see unfolding or the messages received during a psychic reading are not necessarily set in stone. A psychic impression is like a snapshot in time based on the influences present in a person's life at any given moment. Should everything in that individual's life continue as is, this is what the psychic sees as the outcome.

The fact is, however, we all have free will and can change the course of our lives, even if an outcome seems predestined. For example, coming from a family of alcoholics doesn't mean you will become one, even though you may be genetically predisposed. You can choose not to drink.

I'm certain you know of many instances where an individual, possibly even yourself, was able to overcome the odds of their circumstances and rise above them because they CHOSE to change the seemingly inevitable outcome.

The first experience I ever had with a psychic was with a woman named Bonnie. I had never met her, and to this day cannot recall how I obtained her name or phone number. I contacted Bonnie and set up readings for myself and five of my friends, and we agreed to meet at a local park. The day of our readings finally came. I began looking around the park and spotted a lone woman with red hair sitting at a picnic table a little distance away. I walked over to her.

"Bonnie?" I tentatively asked.

The woman looked up at me and replied, "Kass?"

With introductions out of the way, I was invited to sit down. I had no idea what to expect, but what came next shocked me.

Bonnie looked down and away from me. "Before I begin, let me tell you there is a dog here – a golden dog," she said as she began rubbing her lower back, "and she's saying to me 'thank you, thank you-it hurt so bad at the end.'" Bonnie looked up at me, finding tears rolling down my cheeks. Only months before, my golden German shepherd, Jessica, had been put down - she'd had spine cancer.

Bonnie again looked away and continued, "and there's another dog here. A small dog. There's something about the eyes." I started crying even harder. My deceased Shi-tzu, Rags, only had one eye which had a cataract in it. Rags and Jessica had been buddies in this lifetime together.

I didn't need to hear another word from Bonnie to believe in this psychic business, but Bonnie didn't stop there. "They are showing me a beautiful green meadow and telling me that when it's your turn to cross, they will be greeting you to bring you over."

By now I was sobbing almost uncontrollably. I remember looking over at my friends just to try to stop crying. They all had looks of fear and concern on their faces.

After Bonnie finished giving me that information, she looked at me and said, "Let's start your reading." I don't remember anything else she said to me. She didn't need to say another word. What she told me about my dogs was plenty! Since then, I've measured every psychic against her.

In the summer of 2000, my then best girlfriend's 18-year-old son was killed in a horrible car accident. Shortly thereafter, I found I would be moving out of state. My girlfriend wanted to help me look for housing, so we ventured to my soon-to-be new town.

While exploring the town and searching for potential new homes, we saw a flyer posted on a bulletin board. The flyer read "Area's Top Psychic" and showed an article about a woman (I'll call her Z) who had been given that title. My new town was where this top psychic happened to live.

As you can imagine, my girlfriend desperately wanted to connect with her son. The flyer said Z could connect with the dead. We looked at one another and, while we wanted to have a reading with this psychic (she was voted Area's Top Psychic after all!), we hesitated. Z's fee was expensive, but we both felt that for that price, she should be good. We wondered if she would let us share the reading so we could split the cost. We called Z and were told that yes, we COULD share the reading between the two of us. It just so happened that she had an open slot later that day, so we made our appointment. We were both eager to hear what she would have to tell us.

We met with Z and I'm sorry to say, it was probably the worst reading either of us had ever had. Z was unable to connect to spirit in an evidential way, meaning she was unable to receive any information that would indicate to my girlfriend that it really was the spirit of her son. She said she was seeing the image of a fox (something that meant nothing to my girlfriend) and then lectured us on her philosophical beliefs. We were both very disappointed with our experiences.

This was a good lesson for me. Price does not always equal quality. People coming for mediumship readings are searching for comfort. They want to hear from their loved ones, for proof of something beyond death. They are not necessarily wanting to hear your thoughts about life.

A few weeks before my girlfriend and I had gone house hunting and our experience with Z, I'd scheduled a reading with the previously mentioned Bonnie in anticipation of my move. I wondered what she saw for my future. Bonnie said she saw me living in a one level brick house, very similar to a ranch style. During our house hunting expedition, we found only two houses my husband and I could afford, and neither were brick or ranch style.

This reading and the one with Z proved to me that even the best psychics have off days.

Five years after my reading with Bonnie about the brick house, my husband accepted a new position in another state, which meant that we would be moving once again. My husband temporarily moved in with his mother and started his new job while the children and I stayed back in Ohio, getting our home ready to sell. During the times he wasn't at the office, he was searching for a new home for us. He called me one night very excited because he had found the perfect house. It was a single level brick Craftsman style house, and yes, we bought it! Note: Bonnie never told me WHEN I would be living in the brick house, just that she saw me living in one. I had assumed the brick house was relevant to the previous move.

Before retiring, I had a career as a foot reflexologist and owned a holistic healing center. During a session with a new client, I received the following psychic images and impressions: a lighthouse with a sailboat in the water, a short distance from the shore, appearing to be in Maine or somewhere on the east coast. Because of what I saw and the tension I felt in my client's feet, I wondered if she were going on vacation or needed some relaxation time. Relaying this information, she was unable to verify any of it. She was not going on vacation and most definitely was not going to the east coast. She did not own a home on the water, she had never been sailing, nor did she plan to any time in the near or distant future. Strike three for me!

As it happened, about three weeks after this reflexology session, I was going to be hosting an event featuring internationally known medium, James Van Praagh. He was coming to our small conservative southwest Michigan town and the event was sold out. It was all very exciting!

What was **NOT** exciting was this: a week before his appearance, I learned members of Lighthouse Church were going to stage a march in protest of his appearance, this event, and of me.

Two Lighthouse Churches were nearby, but I wasn't sure which one was protesting. I called both offices leaving messages saying I would be happy to answer their questions and discuss any concerns they had. I never got a call back from either of them.

What does this have to do with the vision I saw for the client? The information I had received wasn't incorrect – it was just for me rather than her.

Here is the validation of the message: the lighthouse was Lighthouse Church. The sailboat represented the trinity of Father, Son, and Holy Spirit. (I have since learned a sailboat or a triangle is my symbol for a trinity, whether the Holy trinity or body, mind, and spirit.) The water was the Kalamazoo River, which flowed behind the building where the event was to take place.

I later learned forty men had indeed walked behind the event's venue along the riverfront praying for my soul on the morning of Mr. Van Praagh's appearance.

Many of us have been told or have heard that being psychic is terrible, evil, or of the devil. Nothing could be further from the truth. The purpose of prophesy is to provide guidance, strength, encouragement, and comfort to others. According to the Apostle Paul in 1 Corinthians (14:1), Love is the greatest gift of the Spirit to develop, and the most important spiritual gift to develop after the gift of Love is prophesy.

THOUGHTS FOR CONSIDERATION:

- Make lists of the positives and negatives you know about psychics. Include any words and phrases you may have heard, images you may have seen, and thoughts, feelings, and beliefs you or others may have held or now hold. How do each of these lists make you feel?

- How have your beliefs about psychics changed over the course of your lifetime? Did anything occur to cause this change?

- Has a psychic ever taken advantage of you?

- What was the best psychic reading you've ever had?

- What do you consider to be a good psychic reading?

- What was the worst psychic reading you've ever had?

- What is your favorite psychic reading you've ever given?

- Do you follow a ritual in preparing for a reading, whether giving or receiving?

PSYCHIC GAMES

When practicing the following activities, be aware of **how** and **where** the information comes to you. Notice what the energy surrounding an item, name, or location, feels like. Does it feel thick and dense or airy and light? Is it heavy, sluggish, and oppressive or uplifting and fluid? Does the energy make you feel a certain way either physically or emotionally? Do you hear words or see pictures and images? With enough practice, you will begin to differentiate the subtleties of various emotions, feelings, etc.

In the beginning, you may be tempted to take too much time gathering your impressions, which is only natural. If you take more than a few seconds to answer, it is probable that you are listening to your internal chatter, rather than your psychic signals.

Some of the activities and exercises may be easy for you, while others may be frustrating. Acknowledge your feelings and keep practicing. The more you practice, the stronger your abilities will become and the more accurate you will be. Jot down your findings and observations in your journal. Keep track of your progress as you exercise each of your psychic senses.

PSYCHIC EXERCISE #1

Remove the four aces from a deck of cards, choosing one black and one red ace. Face the two cards upside down and mix them up. Holding your hand over each card, try determining which card is which. You may find holding the card to your heart or third eye chakra makes this exercise easier. Note the FIRST thoughts, feelings, or images that enter your mind.

Does the red ace have a different feel than the black ace? Maybe you see the symbol of the card's suit or hear what the card is. Once you've been able to find the red or black ace with some accuracy, try adding another ace to the mix and repeat the same exercise.

Do your best to not second guess yourself!

Are you able to energetically tell the four aces apart?

PSYCHIC EXERCISE #2

Make a set of cards from cardboard, each card with a different color circle on it - yellow, blue, red, etc. Be sure the cards are the same size and that you are unable to see through them. Take two contrasting color cards such as yellow and blue or green and orange, place them upside down, and mix them up. Energetically try to identify the color on each of the cards. Again, does the yellow card have a different "feel" than the blue card? Did you see the color of the circle in your mind or the image of an object of that color? Notice where and how you receive your information.

When you've gotten good at discerning the difference between two colors, add a third color, a fourth, and so on.

You could also make cards with symbols or pictures of animals, flowers, or cars on them. Be creative.

PSYCHIC EXERCISE #3

You will need a partner for this exercise.

Choose two contrasting colors. Your partner should tell you which two colors you will be choosing from, but not tell you which color they are focusing on. When you're both ready, your partner can say in their mind the color they are focusing on, mentally sending you an image of that color or the image of something in that color. Tuning in psychically to your partner, choose the color they are focusing on.

For example: I say to you, "I'm thinking of orange or purple" while I am focusing on the image of an orange and repeating in my mind "orange, orange, orange." You try to pick up on which color I'm thinking of, orange or purple.

Switch roles with your partner. You may find you're a better sender than a receiver. Remember, not all of us are good at everything, and quite honestly, I am not very good at this exercise! We each have our own strengths. Your job is to discover what yours is.

After some practice, try this same exercise using three colors, then four.

Rather than using colors, try animals. Maybe your partner says, "I'm thinking of an elephant or a mouse." You get a feeling of being heavy or cumbersome and find your partner was thinking elephant; or perhaps you feel small or hear a squeak and find they were thinking mouse. Have fun, mix it up. Pay attention to your unique psychic signals.

You can do this exercise with numbers, food, landscapes, vehicles, and even emotions.

PSYCHIC EXERCISE #4

During the NFL season, I make a list of the Sunday games being played and the teams playing them. Using your psychic senses, try to determine which team will win each game.

I found it easier to feel or sense the winning team when someone else read the team choices to me.

Other ideas for practicing your psychic predictions:

- Winner of other sporting competitions like the Kentucky Derby, playoff games, or Olympic events
- First frost or snowfall of the year
- First 70-degree day of the year
- Baby gender
- Mood of your co-workers (You are only reading the energy surrounding them, not psychic impressions about them.)
- Grocery bill total
- What your spouse will order for dinner
- The song or artist that plays next on the radio

The possibilities for practicing are endless!

TIMING OF EVENTS

The time frame for events can be difficult to pinpoint. In your readings, you may ask what season, month, or day an event has or will take place. How long from now will something occur: a year? a month? Maybe you see "3" or hear the number three. Is it three days? Three months? Try to get clarification. This is also why having a clear understanding of your spiritual symbolism (more on this later) is important. Do you get an image, feeling, or color for a specific day, month, or season?

PSYCHOMETRY

Psychometry is a type of divination that uses touch to psychically access information about a person, place, or thing. Touching the individual or object being read can help the psychic tune into their subject's energy.

For example, as a reflexologist, I gleaned physical information about my clients and their health through touching their feet. As I honed my psychic senses, I found I was able to pick up energetic information about them as well.

During a psychic development class, I was partnered with Diana, a woman I had never met. I soon learned she was married, had suffered a miscarriage in the past, and was currently pregnant.

We were about to practice psychometry. Diana gave me a ring, which I held between my hands. I closed my eyes. The image of a high rise building or a skyscraper with a skeleton draped over it entered my psychic vision. 'Oh, heavens,' I thought to myself. 'Skeletons represent death, don't they? I REALLY don't want to share this with her!'

As I continued to hold the ring in my hands, I received more psychic impressions. A motherly feeling came over me. I knew she was currently pregnant, so that didn't surprise me, but the image of the skeleton did. Did it mean the pregnancy would end in miscarriage or that the baby wouldn't survive? Had the ring belonged to her mother? I didn't know, but I knew what impressions I'd received, and I knew I had to give her that information. I also knew I did NOT want to tell this woman about the skeleton!

I took a deep breath and began to relay to Diana the psychic impressions I had received, including the skeleton, without interpreting them for her. She wasn't upset by any of it. It turned out she and her husband, a first-responder, had been at the 9/11 Memorial in New York City. He'd purchased the ring for her there as a gift for Mother's Day. The ring was made from metal recovered from the Twin Towers which had been destroyed by terrorism on September 11, 2001.

You may receive impressions that are confusing to you but describe them to the best of your ability. Your sitter will determine the relevancy of the message. As Lisa Ko says in her book, *Intuition on Demand*, "you get what you get, and you don't get upset." Trust yourself and trust the psychic impressions you receive.

For the following exercises, you will be reading a series of objects through touch. See what information (color, design, etc.) you can garner psychically **before** looking at them. You may find it is easier to read objects in this way simply because you don't make judgments about them based on their appearances. Should you find it difficult to receive impressions, holding the object to your third eye or heart may help. What additional psychic information can you gain by looking at it?

Remember to activate the energy centers in your palms. (See Energy Field Game #2)

PSYCHIC EXERCISE #5

This can be done as a partner or solo exercise.

Ask your partner to give you a piece of jewelry - it doesn't matter if you can determine what it is through touch, just don't look at it. What psychic impressions do you receive? What additional information can you get by looking at it?

If you get stuck, here are some things to consider: Does it feel old or new? What color is it? What material is it made of? Does it have a unique design or something special about it such as an inscription? Is there a playful or somber energy about it? Who did or does this jewelry belong to? Is there a special story associated with it?

If you'd like to try this as a solo exercise, gather three or four items of jewelry that are the same – rings, bracelets, etc., putting them together in a bag. Again, it doesn't matter that you know what pieces they are. Randomly pick one to read without looking at it. (Call the first item A, the second B, and so on.) Without running your fingers over the item, hold it in your hand, seeing if you can identify the piece by the psychic information it reveals to you. After you've read your items, look to see if the information you received correlates to the pieces.

PSYCHIC EXERCISE #6

Place the images of various animals into separate envelopes. Mix the envelopes up and randomly choose one. Determine what type of animal is in the envelope. Describe what it looks like. Does it have fur, feathers, or scales? Does this creature have any unique markings or defining characteristics? What sound does it make? What climate does it live in?

PSYCHIC EXERCISE #7

Without looking at it, hold a photograph of a friend's pet. In addition to the questions in exercise #6, try to determine its personality traits, quirky behaviors, or unusual habits. Let your friend validate your psychic impressions. You can even try this just by having the name of the pet rather than looking at a photo.

PSYCHIC EXERCISE #8

Hold the photo of an individual, either living or in spirit. There should be only one person in the picture, otherwise you may accidentally read the other individual(s) in the picture.

What impressions do you get about this person? Are they male or female, young or old? Do you get a sense of their appearance and/or personality traits? What is the relationship between them and the sitter? What is their occupation or a hobby they enjoy? Is there a trait or habit about this person that stands out?

Describe the background in the photo. What colors, shapes, or symbols do you receive? Was there a special occasion occurring when this photo was taken?

Take your time. Be mindful of your first impressions. If you get stuck, relax, take a deep breath, and ask spirit for more information.

PSYCHIC EXERCISE #9

Ask someone for the first name of an individual they know well, either living or deceased. What can you pick up about this individual's personality? Pay attention to subtle energetic differences: cheerful, pleasant, and gregarious are similar, yet not the same. If you have trouble getting psychic information to flow, ask for the initial of the individual's last name.

You may find writing the individual's name repeatedly or doodling on a piece of paper helps with receiving the flow of psychic information.

Buildings hold the energies not only of themselves, but also of the individuals who reside, work, or participate in activities that occur within them. The energy of a school resonates differently than that of a library, church, bar, or jail. Consider the homes of two or three of your friends. Do they give off different energetic vibes?

Locations act in the same manner. Cemeteries, sports arenas, zoos, parks, etc. all have unique energetic vibrations, and events that have occurred in these locations will further influence the energy there.

PSYCHIC EXERCISE #10

Visit a variety of buildings and locations and see what psychic information you can gather about them. If you have difficulty, try touching the building or sitting at the location. Verify the information you receive, if possible.

ADDITIONAL THOUGHTS:

Rather than saying, "I don't know why I'm getting _____," try saying "I'm getting _____." When you receive psychic impressions, you are receiving them for a reason. Trust what you see, hear, feel, smell, or seem to know. You aren't making things up!

No one enjoys being wrong, but it's our egos that shame us out of sharing the full picture. Remember Diana's ring? I was afraid of being wrong, and saying the wrong thing, but the information made sense to her, even if it didn't make sense to me. Don't let your ego get in the way. Put it aside - you can pick it back up later.

Always strive to be an evidential psychic, giving as detailed a reading as possible.

Ask spirit for clarification if necessary. Spirit will not let you down.

Learn **YOUR** own personal psychic symbology. What do certain colors, images, or sounds represent to **you**?

Spiritual Symbolism

PSYCHICS AND MEDIUMS receive signs from Spirit that represent persons, places, things, and events. A spiritual catalog of symbols will be unique to every individual; yours will be different than mine. Having a working knowledge of your personal symbology will allow you to give clearer readings by helping you identify the meaning of the messages you receive, as well as distinguishing subtle differences between similar relationships, feelings, and emotions.

As an example, consider the word "marriage." Is there an image or thought that comes to mind? A feeling, sound, or smell? You may see a gold wedding band, hear church bells, or smell roses. That could be your symbol for marriage...or partnership...or commitment.

Here's another example. Even though a son, father, grandfather, and uncle are all male, they each have uniquely different energetic vibrational signatures, and may each conjure up different feelings, images, sounds, and smells.

You will also want to learn to recognize subtle differences in emotions. Irritation, frustration, exasperation, anger, and rage could describe various levels of the same core emotion. You can be irritated, without being angry. You can feel disgusted without feeling nauseous.

Notice how easily the following words can be interchanged or misinterpreted.

loud vs. boisterous vs. aggressive vs. forward vs. bold

anxious vs. hesitant vs. cautious vs. timid

love vs. lust vs. fondness vs. adoration

What follows is a list of words describing people, locations, events, and emotions that you may encounter during a reading. This is not an all-inclusive list. Continue adding to it. Spend some time with each word, and write down what image, sound, smell, etc. comes up for you. This will be the beginning of your personal psychic symbology catalog. Work with no more than five words at a time, otherwise you may overload your senses or become tired, and not receive your psychic symbols clearly. Take no longer than 10-15 seconds for each word. Any longer and you are most likely trying too hard. You may find it useful to have someone read the words to you.

Do your best to not force the symbols and signs to be what you think they should be. Let Spirit offer them to you.

SPIRITUAL SYMBOLOGY LIST:

Mother	Father	Aunt	Uncle
Son	Daughter	Sister	Brother
Cousin	Child	Baby	Teenager
Friend	Best friend	Classmate	
Grandfather/mother	Grt. grandfather/mother		
Marriage	Engagement	Divorce	Separation
Widow	Widower	Boyfriend	Girlfriend
Boss	Enemy	Birthday	Graduation
Young	Old	Rich	Poor
Money	Career	Travel	Retirement
Death	Accident	Suicide	Illness
Anger	Frustration	Quiet	Shy
Romance	Depression	Boisterous	Love
Confusion	Aggressive	Loud	Country
City	Religious	School	Education
Military	Jail	Criminal	Legal

ADDITIONAL FACTORS:

Do the family members on the father's side (paternal) have a different feel than family members on the mother's side (maternal)?

Does the energy of someone who died a long time ago feel differently than someone who passed more recently?

What about seasons and holidays? Months? Days of the week?

PSYCHIC DEVELOPMENT GROUP/CIRCLE

Consistent practice is the quickest way to develop your psychic gifts. Practicing with a trusted friend or with a group of like-minded people is more fun than doing it on your own. Not only will you get support and gain confidence, but you will also learn from one another. Having a psychic workout buddy or group helps keep you accountable to your own psychic growth.

If you can't find a psychic development group (PDG) nearby, consider starting one yourself.

Here are my suggestions for organizing a PDG:

1. Limit the group size to a core group of 6-8 members. This creates a more intimate group plus you will get to know and trust each other and your gifts very well.

2. Adult members (18+) and only those who are serious about developing their skills. No dabblers! I also suggest that if a member misses more than two or three sessions, they excuse themselves from the PDG or you invite them to leave. Life happens - no hard feelings.

3. Meet no less than twice a month but preferably weekly, with each session lasting 1-2 hours. Depending on how often you meet, consider a 12-16-week commitment with the option to join the next set of sessions.

4. Work on psychic fundamentals. Choose one or two exercises from this book or another source to practice at each meeting.

5. As a group, select a facilitator and rotate the position either weekly or monthly.

Develop clear guidelines for the PDG including:

1. Session format: share quick success/struggle stories, brief grounding/meditation, practice exercises, closing.
2. Confidentiality - what happens in circle, stays in circle. Be protective of your circle and its members.
3. Respect each other's skills, gifts, and journeys.
4. Offer uplifting support and encouragement.
5. Keep focused – no cross talking.

Stick to PSYCHIC development during your time together. Mediumship development should be separate.

As your skills increase, you may want to consider organizing separate development groups for beginning, intermediate, and advanced students. An online group can provide additional support.

REMOTE VIEWING

REMOTE VIEWING IS THE gathering of information about a person, place, object, or event from a distance using only psychic senses.

Did you know the U.S. government has used remote viewing to spy on other countries by giving a viewer specific coordinates to focus on and gather information from?

A well-known remote viewing mission was The Star Gate Project. Ret. U.S. Army Chief Warrant Officer Joseph McMoneagle (Stargate Chronicles, Mind Trek) and Ret. Lt. Skip Atwater (Project 8200) are two renowned experts on remote viewing. Lt. Atwater founded the US Army's remote viewing unit in 1977. The Men Who Stare at Goats (2009), based on the book of the same name by Jon Ronson, and Third Eye Spies (2018/2019) are two movies you may enjoy, both involving remote viewing.

One Sunday morning an acquaintance, Francine, called me saying she'd lost her diamond ring and wondered, even though it might be a long shot, could I help locate it psychically. **GULP!** I'd never done anything like that before, but I said I would give it a try. It just so happened that my girlfriend, Kathy, and I were going to be meeting with a couple later that afternoon whose house was having some seemingly paranormal activity, so I was already psychically open.

I asked, "where is Francine's ring?" I saw the image of a tree in the middle of a yard, with a ring of grass about 6 feet in diameter around it. I felt she would find her ring somewhere in that area.

I called her and relayed that information. She confirmed to me that she had mowed her yard the previous day.

A few hours later, Francine called me to report that she had found her diamond ring 6 feet away from the tree in the middle of her backyard.

My paranormal investigating friend, Kathy, and I were going to be exploring the old Mansfield Reformatory site, located in Mansfield, Ohio. It was built between the years of 1886-1910 and was later renamed the Ohio State Reformatory (OSR). All I knew about OSR at that time was that portions of the movie, Shawshank Redemption, had been filmed there. And did I mention it was also supposedly haunted?

Before we went to explore OSR, we sat quietly in my living room to see what psychic impressions we each could get about the location. Here were mine:

1. A rosary - was someone Catholic or religious?
2. Pink - OSR was a men's prison, so this was confusing to me.
3. I felt a slight pressure and twinge of "pain" in my chest. Had someone died of a heart attack or emphysema? Neither was beyond the realm of possibility. People die in prison.
4. I felt as if I were being "pulled" to my right.

We shared our impressions with each other, jotted them down in a notebook, and headed to OSR.

Ohio State Reformatory/Mansfield Reformatory was a fascinating tour, and I wasn't prepared for how foreboding the physical structure was. Originally built as a boys' reformatory school, it was subsequently used as a men's prison from 1896 until 1990.

Seeing the tiers of cells in the prison was difficult. Imagining thousands of my fellow human beings suffering under these conditions was almost unbearable.

Was I able to validate any of my initial psychic impressions?

1. In addition to the men incarcerated at the prison, OSR housed the warden and family, the assistant warden and family, some of the prison's guards, and other staff members.

2. As we approached the residential portion of the facility, to my RIGHT was a pink-tiled bathroom.

3. The warden's wife, Helen, was shot in the chest when a handgun accidentally discharged while she was reaching for her jewelry box on a shelf in a closet in the family's quarters. She died of pneumonia three days later at the nearby Catholic Hospital.

4. Warden Glattke died of a heart attack in his office at the prison in 1959.

Trust your impressions, even if they don't make sense. Share your impressions with a friend. Validate them if possible.

REMOTE VIEWING GAMES
REMOTE VIEWING EXERCISE #1

Before visiting an unfamiliar building, what psychic impressions about it can you receive? What material is the building made of? What color(s) is it? Is there anything unique about the structure such as turrets or arches? What about the inside of the building? Is there a certain room you find yourself drawn to? Describe the contents. It's not uncommon to energetically pick up historical aspects of a site. Validate what your remote viewing revealed to you as best you can.

REMOTE VIEWING EXERCISE #2

Ask a friend to place an item such as a teddy bear or a candle somewhere in their house. They should tell you what the item is, but not its location. Find the location of the object, describing it and any identifying items around it. Is it open and spacious or dark and enclosed? Is it indoors or outdoors? In addition to describing the location, can you describe the hidden item in more detail such as its color, shape, design, or size?

REMOTE VIEWING EXERCISE #3

Ask a friend to place an undisclosed item into a bag. Describe the object. What color(s) or shape do you sense? Is the item soft or hard? Are there letters or numbers on it? Does the item evoke any feelings within you?

Now focus your attention on the bag. Is it plastic or paper? Brown or another color? Plain or decorated?

Where are the bag and the item located?

REMOTE VIEWING EXERCISE #4

Have a friend place several items unknown to you on top of a mantle, dresser, coffee table, or countertop. Describe the items. What are the items sitting on? What room are they in? Describe the room.

REMOTE VIEWING EXERCISE #5

Ask a friend if you can remotely visit them at a specific time, 9 P.M. for instance. At the designated time, see if you can "see" what they are doing, wearing, where they are. Are they alone or with others? Get as much detail as possible and confirm with your friend.

Please note, it is unethical (and a bit creepy) to remotely view someone without their permission, as well as an invasion of privacy.

SPIRIT ART

YOU MAY FIND YOURSELF "drawn" (pun intended) to use art as a way of conveying psychic messages.

Rita Berkowitz is a well-known author and psychic artist who sees and draws those who have passed on to spirit and receives messages to offer their loved ones.

Coral Polge, who passed away in 2001, created spirit portraits through physical mediumship. "I literally feel as if I'm the person I'm drawing," she said. "Size, temperament - all of it becomes part of me, and I try to put down what I feel like rather than anything that I actually see."

Medium Harold Sharp is credited with popularizing the auragraph, a type of spirit art, which is another divination tool and a visual representation of an individual's energy field. It can contain not only colors, symbols, and depictions of psychic impressions within it, but also messages from spirit guides or deceased loved ones.

For an in depth study of Auragraphs, I refer you to Spiritualist and medium Angie Morris (www.angiejmorris.com). She is a wonderful instructor, and her classes are great fun.

AURAGRAPH EXERCISE:

If you can draw a straight line or a circle, you can create an auragraph and it only takes about 20 minutes.

While not the traditional way, this is how I create an auragraph:

1. Trace or draw a circle on a piece of paper. A 6-inch circle is a good size.

2. Decide what creative medium (colored pencils, crayons, chalk, markers) you wish to work with and have them readily available.

3. Ground yourself and connect with your sitter's auric field. Allow all your psychic senses to be present and to come out to play.

4. You may be drawn to use a certain color. Use it. Perhaps the image of the sun or a bird appears. Place it into the circle. If drawing intimidates you, write the word out. (Ex: blue bird, orange falling leaf)

5. Do you get a feeling or emotion when connecting with the sitter's auric field? Can this feeling be represented by a color or symbol? Can you draw it? If not, write the words down.

6. If words or phrases come to you, add them to the aura-graph. I prefer putting words and messages outside the circle.

When I have finished with the auragraph, I like to be silent and allow my sitter to look at it. I feel what they notice is as important as the messages I receive. What stands out for **them**? How do **they** interpret the auragraph? I then continue sharing with them my own interpretation.

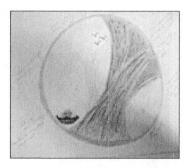

Additional examples of auragraphs I've created are on my website at www.houseofthespirit.org.

The following are examples of other types of spirit art.

Psychic/medium Tina Michelle (www.tinamichelle.com) includes angel drawings with her readings, depicting past, present, and future.

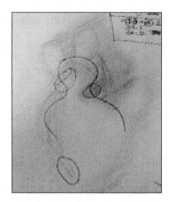

Robyn Adair drew this portrait of my daughter's spirit guide.

Mediumship

MEDIUMSHIP IS THE ABILITY to communicate with those who no longer physically exist on the earthly plane but are now living in spirit. In other words, mediumship means being able to talk with the dead. Should you have the desire and ability to do mediumship work, find a reputable teacher to learn from, and a mentor to guide you.

All mediums are psychic, yet not all psychics are practicing mediums. This is a distinction that can sometimes be difficult to make but is important to remember. A medium can **interact** with someone who is in spirit. A psychic who is **NOT** a medium may gather information and impressions **ABOUT** one who is now in spirit, but not interact with them.

There are various ways individuals can open to their mediumship:

Natural - one who is born with mediumship ability; it seems to have always been there.

Trauma – dormant mediumship abilities that are awakened by experiencing a traumatic event such as a near death experience or the loss of a loved one.

Learned – mediumship abilities activated by learning me-
diumistic skills. This may be done by attending classes
and workshops or even reading books and following the
suggestions given.

No matter how one comes into their mediumship, consistent practice is key to developing and strengthening me-
diumistic ability.

It is important that you not compare yourself with other
mediums. Not all mediums have the same abilities, but they all
communicate with the dead. Take for instance these examples:
Echo Bodine sees a spirit as if they were a real person,
while others may see that spirit within their mind's eye.

Thomas John, known as the Manhattan Medium and
Seatbelt Psychic, is amazingly accurate at receiving the
names of those in spirit, along with detailed information
about them.

Mary Ann Winkowski, the Original Ghost Whisperer,
sees spirits *before* they cross over into the Light. Once
they have crossed over, she can no longer see them.

A medium's main purpose is to:
• Help provide healing and comfort to both the living
  and those in spirit.

- Act as an ambassador to the spirit world, providing a voice for those who've passed.
- Prove continuity of life beyond the grave...we don't die!

As a medium, please do not give unsolicited messages. Always ask permission to give someone a reading.

- Not everyone is a believer in the afterlife or in the Spirit World.
- They may be fearful of death or spirit.
- Not everyone may be open to receiving a message from the deceased, especially if they did not have a good relationship with them.
- They may still be deeply in grief or shock and not ready to receive a message.
- Unless you are invited, you are invading their personal space.

What happens when a spirit comes to you with a message to deliver to someone who is living? Ask the intended recipient if they believe in the afterlife. If they say no, then let it go. If they say yes or maybe, you can ask if they'd like the message.

You could also say "I had a dream last night that...." and deliver the message in that context.

Speaking of dreams - our loved ones will often communicate by visiting in a dream. How will you know if it's just a dream or an actual visit? You'll **FEEL** it, often awakening with a sense of peace or feeling of love. Spirits who have visited me in my dreams also have a distinct sparkle in their eyes.

Jack, the father of a woman I'd been best friends with all through school, came to me in spirit with a message for his daughter, Laura. Laura and I had not seen each other in many years and were no longer close. I told Jack I wasn't willing to contact her because it would be awkward after all the time that had passed between us. Jack wouldn't leave me alone, however, and showed up several more times over the course of three weeks. He was relentless in his persistence! I finally gave in and told Jack I would contact Laura, but he had to leave me be after that. He agreed. I delivered Jack's message to Laura by telling her "I had a dream about your dad the other night. In the dream he said ..." Laura readily accepted the message I gave her and said it sounded like something her dad would say. Jack has not appeared to me since.

I am fortunate to have met some of the industry's top psychics and mediums. I've also seen and been exposed to frauds, as well as psychics and mediums who took advantage of people seeking assistance during their most vulnerable times. When it comes to seeking out a psychic or medium, you must be aware and pay attention to your intuition. Ask for referrals to psychics or mediums from people you know and trust. Always check with your intuition to see if that individual is a good fit for you.

All mediums should strive to be evidential mediums. This means to offer the sitter valid information that would verify the connection with the person in spirit. Names, significant dates, a sense of the spirits' personality, or a shared memory, among other things, could all be considered evidential. In other words, the information should not be generic or applicable to everyone but something of significance between the spirit and the sitter.

There is a phenomenon called "psychic amnesia." This occurs when you cannot take or understand information the psychic or medium is giving you at the time of your reading, only to remember it later. For instance, the medium says they are connecting with a woman who was like a mother to you, she was an aunt, and you stayed summers with her. She taught you to cook and bake and that was your special connection with each other. She passed peacefully in her sleep. The aunt is showing a blue ribbon. The reading is complete, and you can take and understand all the information except the ribbon. Two days later you remember that Auntie Em DID bake award winning apple pies every year for the county fair, something she was very proud of and got a ribbon for.

While the purpose of this book is not to teach you **HOW** to be a medium, the exercises given throughout can help to advance your mediumship.

The following is a good exercise to practice and one of my favorites.

MEDIUMSHIP EXERCISE

Ask a friend for the first name of someone they know who is now in spirit. This should be someone they knew well, not Uncle Ernie who died 40 years ago whom they never met. While you may indeed be able to contact Uncle Ernie in spirit, your sitter will probably not be able to validate the information you receive. If you have trouble connecting, ask for the initial of the spirit's last name.

1. Center and ground yourself.

2. Open your third eye, using any method that works for you. I personally like to envision an on/off button I can press. You

could also imagine a bell or chime, an open/closed sign or even simply say "Let's begin." This lets the spirits know that you are home and are accepting visitors!

3. Ask whomever you are trying to contact to please come forward. You may feel them step into your energy field or they may impress images into your mind's eye. Keep the communication between you and the spirit open. Information can come quickly so stay alert. Ask the spirit for further clarification if necessary.

4. Gather evidential information with the person in spirit such as their relationship to the sitter, their physical description, personality traits, how, when, or where they died. Is there a special memory or a message they want to share?

5. In delivering the information and messages, use the spirit's **exact** words, even if you're uncomfortable with them.

6. Ask if spirit has any other messages they wish to convey before they go.

7. Thank spirit for coming forward.

8. Close your third eye. Press your off button, ring your bell or chime, flip your open/closed sign, or just say "I am finished."

9. Clear your auric field. This can be done by quickly "brushing" the energy off your arms, flicking it off your fingers, imagining raindrops flowing over you, saying "clear me" to yourself, or any other method of your choice.

Our deceased loved ones want to communicate with us just as much as we want to with them. While it can be helpful, you do not need a medium to be able to do so. Speak with them. Rest assured they hear you and with practice, you will hear them. Trust that Spirit will work with you.

WARNING: This next story comes with a few "f-bombs." Skip it if that word offends you.

One evening, my girlfriend asked me to connect with someone who was in spirit named Mark. I heard "brother," but the connection to her didn't feel like a brother. My friend only had one brother, who was most definitely alive, and his name was not Mark. This connection didn't feel like a cousin or uncle either. Oddly enough, it didn't feel like a connection to my friend at all. I was confused and asked for more clarification. My friend told me that she didn't really know Mark, had met him only a couple of times, but that he had been her brother, Tom's, best friend. That information was all I needed.

Mark came forward and I "felt" my body become big and most definitely male, like a "man's man," and very outdoorsy. I felt like I had a big, lusty (lusty was the only way to describe this feeling) appetite for everything: eating, drinking, working, playing, sex. I felt like I was loud and that I had a huge laugh. I heard "I don't fuckin' believe this shit," as if Mark were shocked there was an afterlife. I also heard, "I'm serious as a fucking heart attack. I just don't fuckin' believe this."

In my mind's eye, I saw a very pleasant looking dark-haired man with a wide smile. He was tan and dressed in khaki shorts and a pink polo shirt.

I felt like Mark had fallen and hit his head. I also felt somewhat sheepish and embarrassed. This feeling had something to do with his mom and just being human. I wondered if Mark had died while on the toilet and his mom had found him exposed on the floor, but I was unable to get further clarification from him. He would just shake his head and say, "I don't fuckin' believe this."

Mark said to tell Tom he was sorry they couldn't make their trip together as planned, but to go ahead, and he would join him, even though it would only be in spirit.

He also told Tom to stop drinking and smoking, that he was "serious as a fuckin' heart attack" about this. He said, "I don't fuckin' believe this" one more time and was gone.

I relayed this information to my girlfriend, who passed it on to her brother.

Here was the result:

1. Mark was dark haired and quite handsome.

2. He was the captain of a fishing boat, loved eating and drinking, loved women…and women loved him.

3. He'd had a heart attack while on his boat and died, hitting his head when he fell to the floor.

4. While cleaning out his apartment, his mom found his sex toys.

5. The two friends had been planning a trip to Gettysburg for many years and it was scheduled for the summer Mark died.

6. Mark was fond of using the "f" word, and "serious as a fucking heart attack" was his favorite expression.

7. He had not believed in life after death.

Hearing the term "serious as a fucking heart attack" is what convinced Tom that his friend had indeed come through in spirit. Because of this, Tom quit smoking and cut down on his drinking. After the reading, I was sent a photo of Mark – dressed in khaki shorts and a polo shirt, with pink curtains behind him.

❈ ❈ ❈

The following occurred early on in my mediumship education:

A 9-year-old boy named Trevor was killed in my hometown in a horrible accident. Trevor had ridden his bike into the path of a semi-truck, was struck, and instantly killed. This tragedy shook our entire community. A couple of days later, I was driving past the location where the accident had occurred, and there Trevor was, sitting in the front passenger seat of my car. He had a worried look on his face and said, "I don't know what happened. My mom won't stop crying."

To say I was surprised was an understatement. I had just been driving alone in my car, minding my own business when suddenly I had a passenger. And he was a spirit.

My maternal instinct kicked in and I just wanted to hold him and comfort him. I looked at Trevor and said, "Oh, honey. You were in a bad accident. Your mom is crying because you died and she's really, really sad."

Trevor quietly said, "Oh, I see…" and he disappeared.

I was a little unnerved by what had just taken place. I had a very intense, strong urge to contact Trevor's mom to tell her what had just happened. I felt it was my "job." However, I was warned not to and I'm glad I heeded that advice.

1. I had no business intruding on Trevor's mother's grief, no matter how well-meaning my intentions would have been.

2. I was a stranger to this family. I was not invited into their circle, nor was I asked to contact Trevor on his family's behalf.

3. I believe this incident occurred for Trevor's benefit. He needed to understand what was going on and I was able to provide him with the answer.

You cannot save the world nor is it your job to do so.

OTHER MEDIUMSHIP OPPORTUNITIES:

A group of people gathered in one space to receive messages from a medium is known as a gallery reading. While not everyone in attendance receives a direct message during these events, the healing and messages of hope given are wonderful to witness. Many mediums offer gallery readings. Look for an opportunity to attend one in your area.

Demonstrations of mediumship are often part of Spiritualist church services. Additionally, they may provide opportunities for studying mediumship.

There are many Spiritualist communities around the world you can visit, but the most well-known one in the

United States is Lily Dale. Located in northwestern New York state, it has been in existence since 1879. Well known persons such as Susan B. Anthony, Elizabeth Cady Stanton, Wayne Dyer, and Thomas John, as well as lesser known talented individuals have spoken and presented there.

At Lily Dale you can receive private healings and psychic readings, listen to lectures, attend workshops, church services, and so much more. Throughout the day, Lily Dale offers free healing services and demonstrations of mediumship. The Lily Dale property is soothing for the soul, with the energy there both palpable and powerful. If you've never been, put Lily Dale on your bucket list and go. If you have been before, visit again.

SPIRIT DEVELOPMENT CIRCLE

Another way to develop your mediumship is by sitting in spirit development circles. The following aren't rules, but simply guidelines and are suggestions taken from First Spiritual Temple. Some have been modified.

1. Choose no more than six individuals who are serious about developing their mediumship. Select a spirit circle leader.

2. Pick a day, time, and location where you will consistently meet, and ideally meet once a week.

3. Participants should arrive 10-15 minutes early (this helps to slough off the cares of the day) and be ready to work at the designated time. Late arrivals are not allowed. Remember that you are making an appointment with Spirit. Spirit will be on time as should you.

4. Plan on sitting in the spirit circle for at least an hour but not longer than 75 minutes.

5. Seating is arranged in a circle and participants should be in the same seat each session unless the leader feels a shift in energy is necessary. Additionally, there may be times when new people join the spirit circle or members leave or are unable to attend.

6. Include the following elements in the spirit circle:

~ Opening thoughts/prayer
~ Call to God, Spirit, Creator, or Higher Power
~ An exercise, music, or song to raise the vibration of the individuals in the room
~ A period of receiving messages from Spirit
~ Closing thoughts/prayer

7. At the conclusion of the spirit circle, participants should leave the area, perhaps going to another room.

8. Developing mediumship requires patience, discipline, hard work and study, and commitment.

Other considerations:

1. Do not offer refreshments before the meeting as it tends to encourage chitchat. If you want to socialize, do so afterward.

2. Record in a notebook the messages that are received.

3. Spirits may be loved ones of those in the circle, but they may also be unknown to anyone. (I once had Don Cornelius, creator of the TV program Soul Train, appear to me to say he'd "made it and was doing fine." He had died from suicide.)

4. Once the spirit circle is closed, give no more messages.

5. Do not discuss the spirit messages received during the spirit circle. This could potentially foster dialogue and inadvertently influence messages received at the next meeting. In other words, what happens in circle, stays in circle!

6. Refrain from sharing information about your loved ones in spirit as they may appear in future circles with a message for you. You don't want that message influenced by anything you may have said to another participant.

7. Continue to study mediumship and other related topics.

8. Have fun! While developing mediumship is serious business, serving spirit is a joy.

Tips For Giving
and Receiving A Reading

FOR THE SITTER:

1. Check out the psychic or medium. Are they reputable? Do you get a good feeling about them or does something feel just a little off? Not every psychic or medium will be a good match for you. Do your research and trust your gut. Get a referral from someone you trust.

2. Ground and center your energy. Having a reading is exciting but for some, can be a little scary, especially if it's the first time. You do not want your energy to be scattered.

3. Invite your angels, guides, and loved ones to join you. Ask for any messages from them to come forward through the psychic/medium.

4. Enter the reading with an open mind and willing heart. It's one thing to be discerning, but if you are going to be completely

skeptical and closed off, why bother? The psychic will convey the information and messages they receive for you. A medium should be able to provide evidence of spirit connection.

5. To optimize your time, be prepared with at least three questions you would like to ask the psychic. Psychics are not mind readers.

6. During the reading, do NOT feed the psychic/medium information! In other words, respond with only yes/no, "I don't understand," or "I don't remember" answers. If the reader asks for more information or clarification, be brief. There is a natural tendency to want to fill silences and to tell your story, but please don't. Be okay with long pauses while information is being gathered from the spirit world.

7. A medium cannot force someone in spirit to come forward. For instance, you may want to hear from your mom during your reading, but your dad shows up instead. His message may be the one you needed to hear. Perhaps your dad needed to be in contact with you for HIS healing and growth. It is also possible, as happened to me once, your loved one is "too busy" and doesn't have time to chat! Remember, people in the spirit world are still people and have a life they are living beyond this earthly plane.

8. Many mediums suggest waiting at least 6 months after the passing of a loved one before attempting to contact them. This allows for a time of grieving and adjustment to take place on both sides. Do what is right for you.

9. Limit distractions. This doesn't mean you must have complete silence throughout your reading, but you should turn off the TV/radio. Silence your phone. Is there roadwork occurring outside your window? Close the window.

Try to schedule your reading during a time when family won't be asking for dinner or a snack. Go into another room where you won't be disturbed by other people or pets.

10. Do not come to a reading in an altered state of mind. The psychic will be reading your energy and you do not want yours clouded with alcohol or chemicals.

11. If you sign up for a reading, only you should attend, unless you've cleared it with the reader. Do not bring a friend along at the last minute and ask if they can sit in with you.

12. Take everything with a grain of salt. You have free will. What a psychic sees for you is not written in stone. You can choose to follow a psychic's advice/messages or not.

FOR THE READER:

1. Ground and center your energy. Take a few deep breaths. As you inhale, breathe in peace, calmness, serenity, and love. As you exhale, release tensions, busyness, self-doubt. Feel your physical body relaxing.

You may wish to say a prayer for the highest good for both you and your client and ask that all messages be received and conveyed clearly. Invite your angels and guides to join you, along with your clients' angels and guides.

2. Not every client will be a good match for you, and that's alright. If necessary, refer them to someone who might be better suited to provide them services.

3. Limit distractions. You may choose to have soft music playing in the background. This can help relax both you and your sitter.

4. Do not give a reading while in a chemically induced altered state of mind, tired, or ill. You also have the right to refuse to do a reading if a client comes to you in such a state.

5. Raise your energetic vibration so you can connect with the spirits' higher vibration. One way to do so is to sing or listen to an upbeat, inspiring song. *(Your Love Keeps Lifting Me)*

Higher and Higher by Jackie Wilson is one of my personal favorites, but even singing *Happy Birthday* will work.

6. Consider sharing "what to expect from a reading" with your client when they book their reading or have this on your website.

DIVINATION TOOLS

DIVINATION, IN ITS PUREST sense, is seeking knowledge and information by seemingly mystical means. There are hundreds of divination tools and techniques available to you ranging from the throwing of bones to the use of dowsing rods.

You have likely been exposed to or even participated in divination methods since childhood. Most of us have seen The Wizard of Oz and watched as Dorothy's image appeared in the witch's crystal ball. You may have even used a Ouija board or chanted "Bloody Mary" three times into a mirror in a darkened room, hoping to see an image and yet being afraid you might.

A sampling of divination tools are:
- Tarot cards and oracle decks
- Pendulums and dowsing rods
- I-Ching
- Crystal balls, scrying mirrors, or other reflective surfaces
- Tea leaves, coffee grounds

- Bones and Rune stones
- Talking/divination boards (Ouija, angel)
- Candle work, crystals
- Numerology and astrology

These are all wonderful tools to use, but divination tools are just that: tools. In and of themselves, they hold no power. Like a vehicle, they require an operator to work. Their purpose is to act as a conduit for guidance, direction, and insight. When you add your own intuitive interpretation to the messages they reveal, the reading is taken to another level.

THOUGHTS FOR CONSIDERATION:

- What divination tools have you used? Do you have any favorites?

AUTOMATIC WRITING

AUTOMATIC WRITING IS A divination tool, but also a form of channeling. It can assist you in receiving messages for yourself or others by accessing the wisdom of the Higher Self, guides, angels, or other etheric entities, as well as Spirit itself. And, in the case of mediumship, someone in spirit.

Automatic writing is easily done by allowing yourself to enter a state of relaxation or light trance and being open to receiving messages or answers to a specific question. It's normal to wonder whether you are really receiving messages or are just making it all up. TRUST YOURSELF. Automatic writing will help take you out of your logical mind and open your psychic senses.

The following is an example of an automatic writing session I did for myself when I was experiencing a bout of depression. Question to my Higher Self: "How can I overcome this depression?"

Reply: "Turn it over, turn it over, turn it over. Do the hard thing. Trust that all is fine-you have protection and that's really your question, how can you get through this. You are so loved…keep speaking, keep reaching, keep living. DONE."

The reply to my question of how to overcome the depression came quickly, and when the reply was complete, I heard "DONE!" in my psychic ear.

The answer was short and simple and to the point. The message from Spirit was clear and rang true to me.

Automatic writing sessions need not involve a lot of time; 10-15 minutes is probably sufficient.

Use automatic writing to gain information for a sitter. For instance, John is seeking guidance regarding his career. You can ask for connection to John's Higher Self. Following the steps for automatic writing, you ask the question, "what does John need to know about his career?" Let the words and sentences flow.

AUTOMATIC WRITING GAMES
AUTOMATIC WRITING EXERCISE #1

1. Relax, take a deep breath in and fully exhale. Repeat until you feel grounded and centered.

2. Have a question to which you would like an answer to or clarity on such as "why am I afraid to…" or "how do I move beyond…"

3. Set a timer. Five minutes is a good length of time to begin with.

4. As answers/messages begin to flow, start writing.

5. Do not interpret or edit, just write. Be aware that your mind will try to distract you or stop you by chattering and reacting to what you are writing.

6. Keep writing.

7. Trust Spirit and trust yourself.

8. When you are finished, you are finished.

AUTOMATIC WRITING EXERCISE #2

Do an automatic writing session for a friend, connecting with their Higher Self to find an answer or insight into a question they may have.

AUTOMATIC WRITING EXERCISE #3

Take a walk in a park or the woods. Find a tree that you feel drawn to. Sit next to it, perhaps even leaning your back against it. Take in a couple of cleansing breaths and ask the tree for its wisdom either for a specific situation or a general message.

Perhaps you get more clarity near water or in a field of flowers. Find a special place in nature, one you feel drawn to.

Don't limit yourself. Journal the messages you receive. Write about any feelings or emotions you experience.

Ethical Responsibility

ON A RECENT TRIP to a psychic expo with friends, I was asked which psychics I recommended they see. I suggested they walk around the booths to find who they were energetically drawn to.

Why didn't I tell them which psychics to see? They needed to listen to and trust their own intuition about what was best for them. We are each on our own path and must follow our own guidance from Creator.

Do not allow anyone to become dependent on you or to become anyone's psychic guru. Although insight from an outside source can be valuable, especially during times of grief or crisis, each one of us needs to learn to rely on our own intuition for answers.

Some psychics will only read the same client once every six months unless a specific occurrence such as a health concern, job change, or other life altering situation arises. This helps prevent the client's dependency on you. Ask your intuition and decide what your psychic reading policy will be.

Just a word of caution: While there are wonderful readers, practitioners, and vendors at psychic events, not everyone in attendance has your best interest at heart. I've been appalled by some individuals that will take advantage of vulnerable attendees searching for helpful advice, services, and products and, in turn, by attendees blindly allowing themselves to be taken advantage of. I don't mean to be critical…I've fallen victim to some of these predators myself, but you must use your intuition and common sense to guide you. It's a red flag if something feels off.

There was a popular vendor that everyone raved about who, for decades, was a staple at psychic expos and metaphysical events around the country. His energy always made me feel extremely uncomfortable, so I avoided his booth. It was confusing because I didn't share the positive feelings about him that others did, but I couldn't change that, and I didn't try to. In the autumn of 2020, this individual was arrested on "two counts of rape and seven charges of gross sexual imposition" which allegedly took place over a thirteen year span.

The moral of the story: don't be afraid of searching for answers and always trust your intuition!

If you do attend a psychic expo or other such event, be sure to ground yourself before you go, and if necessary, throughout your time at the event. The energy there can be overwhelming!

Most people seek out psychics to learn about their future concerning love or relationships, children and family, career, and finances, all of which are extremely important in any of our lives. They are entrusting the psychic with their energetic heart, and as a psychic, you are happy to be of service and offer insight and guidance to them.

As a psychic, you have an ethical responsibility to:

- Do no harm.
- Gather information psychically and relay that information as clearly to your sitter as possible.
- Be neutral, compassionate, and non-judgmental.
- Be clear minded when doing a reading.
- ALWAYS maintain your client's confidentiality.
- Do not allow anyone to become dependent on you.
- Be the best psychic you can be by continuing to develop your abilities.

SHARING "BAD" NEWS

Knowing that you need to trust the psychic information you get for a sitter, how do you share bad news? Thoughtfully, gently, and tactfully.

Most psychics I know will not give messages about infidelity or death to a client, and I agree with this. Some psychics even begin their readings by stating such. Your words hold power and giving negative information without facts can bring about irreparable harm…divorce, suicide, etc.

I was in the lobby of my holistic healing center waiting for my client to emerge from the treatment room after her session with me. At the same time, Jane, a young woman who was just beginning to give psychic readings happened to be standing in the lobby waiting for her practitioner.

My client came out, paid for her session, and left. Jane said to me, "Oh, my God, she has cancer, doesn't she?" "No, not that I know of," I replied. Even if my client had cancer, I wouldn't have divulged that information due to confidentiality.

Jane insisted that my client did indeed have cancer, that she saw it all throughout her aura, which she said was gray. She also told me I needed to tell my client. I said nothing to my client and ten years later, she is still here, never having had cancer.

Can you imagine the anguish I might have caused had I shared the information? First, the client never asked about her health so to have given that information would have been an intrusion. Secondly, the information was incorrect.

A woman once asked me for a reading concerning her rebellious, 17-year-old daughter. She was disrespectful to her mother, destroyed property whenever she came home, and was involved with an older man who her mother did not approve of. Because of this disapproval, she would be gone for long periods of time, only coming around when she needed money or a place to stay. The mother was afraid her daughter would end up dead and wondered what I saw.

I saw the daughter involved in heavy drinking and drug usage, and that the boyfriend was influencing her poor choices. I didn't see she was going to die, but I did see her life being very difficult. This behavior would persist for several years, during which time, she would become pregnant, and the boyfriend would not stick around.

Validations: The daughter had, indeed, become involved with drugs and alcohol, the boyfriend was verbally and emotionally abusive, they lived in a car, and she became pregnant. She refused her mother's offer to live at home because the boyfriend was not welcome there. Once the baby was born, he abandoned them, and she moved back home.

Although it took many years, the last update found their relationship much improved. She is now happily married with three daughters and they own a beautiful home.

The point of this story is, I did not want to tell this woman her daughter would be doing drugs and become pregnant, or that things were not going to get better for quite a while. But I had to, and I did it as delicately as I could.

CHARGING FOR YOUR SERVICES

Many people think psychics should do their work for free since psychic ability is a "gift from God." Please remember you are charging for your time, not your gift. You cannot take a weekend class or read a book and then consider yourself a professional psychic. You have invested considerable time and effort toward developing your skills and you deserve to be compensated. Even clergy get paid for services rendered.

Check the going rate in your area and confirm with your intuition what to charge.

REFERRALS

There will be times when you are not the best healer, psychic, or medium for an individual. Don't take it personally - it has nothing to do with you or your abilities. It's just not the right energetic mix. Refer them to someone who might be a better fit. After all, a client's well-being is your top concern.

Likewise, there will be times when a client needs help beyond a psychic reading. Gather a list of therapists and counselors, healers such as body and energy workers, and traditional medical practitioners in your area.

Have phone numbers readily available for local sexual assault, domestic violence, mental health, and suicide crisis lines, and any other organizations you feel could be useful. A list of national hotline numbers is at the back of this book.

OTHER PSYCHIC SHENANIGANS

I went to dinner one evening with two other women who were attending the same conference in Washington, D.C. that I was. As we walked down the street, we noticed a shop offering psychic readings for $15, and decided to see what the psychic inside could tell us. We determined I would be read first. As I always do, I said a prayer of protection, not because I was frightened or nervous, but because I wanted to have only the truth revealed to me. The psychic told me I had a connection to Russia, which was true. My husband and I had hoped at one time to adopt a child from there. She was unable to provide me with any further information.

Terri went next for her reading. It was very generic, but nothing out of the ordinary.

When Karen's reading was over, she was quite disturbed. She'd been told a curse had been placed on her, but for $200, the psychic could get rid of it. Despite our best efforts to discourage her, she went back the next day and paid the fee, only to be told the curse was much worse than originally believed. And surprise - it would cost additional money to fully "free" her.

Please be careful not to fall for scams such as this. **NEVER** pay to have a curse removed. In fact, run as fast as you can from anyone who asks you to do so.

COLD READING

Psychic readings are based on energetic information being received about the sitter. Cold reading picks up on subtle visual cues unknowingly given by a sitter such as body language, the presence or absence of a wedding ring, etc. rather than obtaining information psychically. For this reason, many psychics look away from the sitter when giving readings - they don't want to inadvertently slip into this practice. It's also why many psychics prefer doing readings over the phone and do so with great success.

There will be times when your psychic connection is just not up to par – you're human after all. Do not allow yourself to fall back on cold reading, which can be easy and tempting to do especially when you feel stuck. You may not even be aware you are doing it.

Sadly, there are some psychics who knowingly resort to cold reading when they are unable to get psychic information rather than admitting they are having an off day or are unable to connect with the sitter. Not only is this cheating, but it's unfair to the sitter.

There are also times when a psychic will "fish" for information by asking the sitter questions. As previously mentioned, do not provide the psychic with any leading information. They should be able to clearly describe and relay the impressions and information they are receiving. Remember – while it's human nature to want to be helpful, this is not the time. Do not try to make the reading fit.

PARANORMAL INVESTIGATION

YOU MAY WISH TO DELVE into paranormal investigation using your psychic abilities, and many people do. Paranormal investigators can offer relief and reassurance to folks who believe their homes or properties are haunted. Kathy Conder, founder of Michigan Paranormal Encounters, (MPE), is one of the best investigators I know. She also is one of my closest friends and is the Kathy I've mentioned many times earlier in this book. You would never guess by looking at this quiet, soft-spoken woman that some of her favorite things to do are traipsing through cemeteries, sitting in dark, dank basements, or wandering through abandoned jails and historic battlefields, searching for spirits.

Kathy has decades of experience and a vast knowledge of the paranormal field. We've done countless investigations together, both as a duo and as part of the MPE team. Despite what television programs would lead you to believe, paranormal investigation is not necessarily exciting. It's a lot of sitting around in creepy basements or dusty box-filled attics. In the dark. Silently. Waiting...and waiting.

Alleged paranormal activity can almost always be explained by things such as ley lines, faulty wiring, critter infestation, overactive imaginations, drug usage, or mental instability.

Even if none of the above reasons are the cause, you will find most hauntings are not actually active hauntings. Instead, they are the result of an energetic imprint caused by the etheric body. The etheric body is one of the subtle bodies and is the holographic image of the physical body that the soul has taken as incarnate. This could explain the reason people see ghosts.

A ghost is not the same as someone who is in spirit. You cannot interact with a ghost because it's a holographic image. These holographic images may be seen for seconds, days, or years after the passing of an individual, depending on how long the soul feels it necessary.

You can, however, interact with a spirit, and that would be considered an active haunting.

Locations where sudden violent and horrific incidents have occurred often have energetic loops. That is to say, the imprint from the incident replays over and over and will continue to do so until the energy of that event has run out. This can explain why battlefields, hospitals, jails, and prisons seem to be so paranormally active.

The Battle of Gettysburg is considered one of the bloodiest battles ever to have taken place on American soil. Over a three-day period, there were 51,112 casualties: 7,058 killed, 33,264 wounded, 10,790 missing and captured, along with 1,500 horses and mules killed. There have been numerous sightings reported of soldiers, both Union and Confederate, appearing seemingly out of nowhere and then disappearing. There have also been observations of battles being played out, an overpowering smell of gunpowder, blood, and death, the sounds of hoofbeats and gunshots or cannons being fired, and an overwhelming feeling of despair. It's no wonder Gettysburg is considered so paranormally active, given the horrific brutality and intensity of that event. But is there true paranormal activity occurring or are the sightings the result of holographic images? Maybe it's a combination of both. Eventually, the holographic images will fade, but it will take a very long time. This, perhaps, explains why investigators have been unsuccessful in crossing these seemingly lost souls over to the Light. The spirits of the soldiers really aren't present, they are holographic images. Just a thought.

Kathy received a call from a woman named Susan whose childhood home was experiencing strange occurrences. Although she no longer lived in the house, she was trying to get it ready for sale, and was afraid to be there alone. We decided to meet with Susan to gather preliminary information and see if a full investigation by the MPE team was warranted.

Driving down a gravel road for some distance and arriving at the given address, we were greeted by the sight of an enormous old farmhouse which looked as if it hadn't been lived in for many years. The lawn was woefully neglected as well. This, combined with the fact that there were no neighbors within miles, made it seem the perfect setting for a horror movie. A dark, dusty old house, even in the daylight, can appear ominous and frightening, your mind ready to imagine the worst.

Susan met us at the back door and invited us in. Kathy and I wandered the house and property separately. Each poorly lit room displayed peeling paint and wallpaper, and many rooms had graffiti scrawled on the walls. There was evidence of mouse and squirrel infestation, which was especially noticeable in the kitchen. The house emitted an overall uneasy feeling of sadness.

In my mind's eye, while walking around the backyard and outbuildings, I was struck with the unpleasant image of some type of animal abuse. I could smell blood, and I felt physically nauseous.

When it was time to come back together, we sat on the back porch and gave Susan our initial findings. Kathy shared first while I mentally wrestled with how to broach the subject of the animals.

When the gazes of the two women turned to me, I took a deep breath and said I felt something very bad involving animals had occurred here and pointed to the area where I felt it had taken place. While disgusted inwardly, I did not let my feelings show. I relayed the information as factually as I could without passing judgment. Susan acknowledged her brother had indeed been involved in animal cruelty, and he had spent time in an institution for antisocial behavior.

Kathy and I were investigating the location of what used to be a hospital in southwest Michigan. Legend stated the notorious criminal, Al Capone, would bring his men to this hospital when they required medical intervention while in the area. The hospital was reported to have tunnels leading from its basement to the river behind it, which was how Capone and his men were able to travel in and out of town undetected.

After the hospital closed, the building was purchased by a local civic organization who occupied it for quite some time before selling it to a private individual, where it sat empty and dormant for many years.

Employees of the civic organization witnessed chairs and dishes being moved about, lights being turned on and off, strange noises, sightings of spirit children, and a host of other unexplained occurrences happening in the building. Repairmen in the building reported being tapped on the shoulder by unseen fingers or having their work tools tampered with, especially when they were in the basement. In fact, paranormal activity occurred so frequently that many employees and service workers refused to be in the building alone.

Kathy and I not only investigated this location together privately on many occasions but led public and private group investigations there as well. During one group investigation, I decided to sit in one of the rooms alone to see what impressions I could get. To my surprise, a spirit doctor appeared, complete with lab coat and stethoscope. A few moments later, a couple of investigators entered the room, setting up their recorders and flashlights, and bringing out a small rubber ball. I sat quietly, the spirit doctor standing beside me, and observed as the investigators asked, "if there are any spirits here, please move this ball." I heard the doctor indignantly reply, "I'm a damn doctor. Why the hell would I play ball with you?" And off he went in a huff.

The doctor was right. These investigators meant no harm, but they were condescending. Would you ask a living doctor to play ball with you? Always speak to those in spirit the way you would speak to them if they were alive and right in front of you.

As of this writing, the building and property is being restored. Kathy still leads public investigations there.

I accompanied Kathy on an interview and preliminary investigation at an assisted living facility. Nurses reported disturbing activity in the basement and were afraid to go down there alone, instead doing so only in pairs. This may come as a surprise to you, but I do not like to be scared. And there are two things that scare me. Clowns and basements. While Kathy spoke to the woman in charge, I made my way into the basement and had a look around. I was grateful it was daylight.

Kathy soon joined me, and we sat in a spot that gave us both chills. Within minutes, a sweet-faced heavyset man appearing to be in his late thirties psychically presented himself to me. While my head didn't ache, there seemed to be a thickness about it, and my thoughts felt fuzzy and slow, like they were flowing through molasses. I wondered if he had been in a coma. I shared this with Kathy.

After trying to communicate with him so we could assist his spirit in moving on to the Light, it became obvious he didn't understand us. I had not previously noticed that this man appeared to have Downs Syndrome along with severe mental deficiencies.

We discovered he liked playing pranks on people because it made him laugh when he scared them. He wasn't being mean, he just thought it was funny. While he was comfortable being in the basement, we knew his spirit didn't belong there. He needed to leave.

We tried asking him to look for a grandmother or grandfather, but that didn't work. It then occurred to me that perhaps there had been a favorite pet that could help.

"Can you see a dog?" I asked.

"Doggie," he replied, and began clapping his hands.

"Go get your doggie," I said, using his terminology, and off he went into the Light, that quickly and that simply.

A follow-up to this location found no paranormal activity occurring after our visit, and everyone finally felt safe to go into the basement. Even alone.

Humans tend to fear and demonize that which we don't understand or can't fully explain. Many people blame unexplained activity in their homes on malevolent spirits or demonic entities. As stated before, most seemingly paranormal activity can be explained logically. You've heard the saying, "all that glitters is not gold." Remember - just because something may scare you, that doesn't mean it's evil. Of the many investigations I've attended, none of them has had a demonic presence.

Just as there are nasty people who walk among the living, there are also nasty spirits. People do not automatically receive halos and angel wings upon their passing. The majority of spirits you will encounter will not be malicious or purposefully cause you pain or suffering. Consider this: there are far more dead people than living and if they really wanted to hurt you, they could and would. Most of us are unable to see spirits so we would be helpless against them should they choose to cause us harm.

I found early on that I did not particularly like the actual process of investigating. What I really enjoyed was assisting those in spirit, when they were present, which was rare.

I personally do not believe people in the spirit world get stuck or are earthbound. As previously mentioned, they have free will and can choose to be here. This doesn't mean some spirits might not be a little confused, especially if their death was sudden or unexpected. Some spirits may be hesitant to move on from this plane because of the beliefs they held here on earth, such as fear of going to hell or being harshly punished for their perceived sins or wrongdoings. They can also be held here by the deep grief of loved ones they are leaving behind or their own hesitancy to leave their earthly loved ones, but those in spirit belong on the other side. Spirits may simply be anxious about what to expect, having never died before. You can assure them a host of others in spirit are waiting to welcome them to the other side and will help them adjust. They will not be alone.

You will find that some people like having spirits around and really don't want them to leave, especially if the spirit is a loved one. Spirits do not belong here on the earth plane. They now live in the spirit world and have things to do there. Can they come to visit? They most certainly can and may do so at any time they desire because, while they no longer have a physical body, they still have free will.

PARANORMAL INVESTIGATION ETIQUETTE AND TIPS:
- Do not make up evidence or embellish your findings. Kathy and I have often gone into situations where we felt "set up" and there was either no actual paranormal activity, or the level of activity was exaggerated.

Be truthful with yourself and your client. You may be disappointed with your findings or lack thereof perhaps, but your integrity will remain intact.

- Respect the property you're investigating. It is disheartening I must even mention this, but I've seen many investigators laughing and carrying on, treating an investigation as entertainment. Many public places have been vandalized by investigators or trash has been left behind. Investigating can be fun and you *should* have a good time doing it but be mindful.

- Respect the property owner. Do not dismiss or downplay their concerns. Many people are truly frightened by what they believe is the occurrence of paranormal activity. You must be able to reassure them that they aren't imagining things, and that everything will be alright.

- Offer the homeowner ways they can energetically clear and cleanse their property. It is more effective that they do it rather than someone else. Lend assistance when necessary. Ideas for clearing and cleansing locations and items are listed at the back of the book.

- Never antagonize or taunt the spirits. Not because they might harm you, but because you should never treat anyone, living or dead, in that manner. Should you meet with an actual spirit during an investigation, talk with them. Find out who they are and why they are there. Encourage them to leave that location and step into the Light. They no longer belong on the earth plane except to visit, which they may do any time they'd like.

• After ruling out possible explanations for psychic disturbances such as faulty wiring, or critter infestation, determine if what is being experienced is actual paranormal activity or psychic residue. Equipment such as cameras, recorders, and KII meters, as well as items such as dowsing rods and pendulums can lend validation to what your psychic senses reveal.

• Try remote viewing to gather psychic impressions of the location you are going to investigate before you arrive, writing them down in a notebook so you can refer to them later. As you proceed with your investigation, jot down additional impressions you receive. You may not be able to validate or confirm the information at that moment but trust yourself and your psychic senses.

• Although you can do it on your own, I feel it's important to investigate with at least one other individual or as part of a team whenever possible. Join a reputable group in your area. If none exists, start your own. As a practical matter, there is safety in numbers. Investigations often find you wandering through dark hallways and unfamiliar territory. Should an accident occur, you will not be alone. Logistically, more area can be covered in less time when you investigate with others.

ANIMAL COMMUNICATION

SPIRIT CAN AND DOES communicate with us through animals. Cardinals, butterflies, and dragonflies are commonly thought to be messengers of deceased loved ones letting us know they are near.

All creatures have lessons to teach us - from the lowly mosquito to the powerful grizzly bear; from dogs and cats to birds and rats; from insects to reptiles, to the feathered, scaly, and furry. Every creature, whether on land, in sea or sky, has a message or a lesson to share with us. You need only to observe and be open to receiving.

Have you ever watched squirrels busying themselves gathering nuts? Perhaps their busyness is a reminder for you to prepare for the future. Squirrels are also very social and playful. Maybe you need to play more or not take yourself so seriously. Maybe you play too much and don't prepare for what lies ahead.

Take special note when an animal appears in your dreams, an uncommon place, or in an unusual way such as its image on a billboard, the side of a bus or truck, or even in a book. Spirit is **REALLY** trying to get your attention!

No matter how an animal shows up in your life, look for the message and teaching it has to offer you. Also pay attention to things such as the landscape, atmosphere, and season as they can be part of it as well.

On a trip to Minnesota, my friends and I stopped to stretch our legs and fill the car up with gas. They went inside while I pumped fuel. Afterward I began to clean the windshield and noticed the biggest, most beautiful, bright green grasshopper I had ever seen sitting on the hood of my car. He was easily 3 inches long.

To have this grasshopper show up in this way had to be a message for sure. After a few moments of enjoying his company, I thanked him for coming and said I needed to leave. He didn't budge. I put my hand next to him. He didn't move. Once again, I told him I needed to go and that he should leave. Still nothing happened. I got into the car and started it up. Surely, he'd get the message, but no, he stayed right where he was, clearly having more to say.

When my companions returned, we decided to go down the street for lunch. The grasshopper remained on the hood of the car all the way to the restaurant. I got out and spoke with him again. He turned to face me. We shared a "moment" between us, and I headed into the restaurant. When I came out, the grasshopper was gone.

According to the classic book, *Animal Speak* by Ted Andrews, when grasshopper appears to you, 'there is about to be a new leap forward in your life.' The appearance of Grasshopper is also a message to trust your own instincts.

Not only were my friends and I in Minnesota visiting with another friend, but I was also checking out a city where my husband had applied for a job. Soon after this trip, my husband accepted a job offer. We were also about to become empty nesters as none of our children would be moving with us. It was a huge leap indeed!

We all can talk with animals. It takes patience and practice. Rather than words, images and pictures are typically used to convey messages between species. Interacting with animals or creatures with a hive mentality, such as ants or bees, may require you to communicate with them collectively rather than individually as you would a dog, cat, or horse.

As an animal communicator, you will be able to provide insights into certain behaviors of animals, and perhaps even assist in finding lost pets.

When my sons were younger, we would often go to the state park, where we would try to call deer to us. Sitting very still, we would whisper and, in our minds say to the deer, "Please come to us. We won't harm you. We only want to see you." Within a few minutes, a deer would arrive. We then practiced calling more deer, asking for two to appear. Two deer would come. We never did get beyond three deer coming near us at one time. There was something magical about being able to communicate with the deer and helping my sons learn to calm their minds and energies enough so that the deer trusted them and would make an appearance.

Using this same technique, we also practiced calling butterflies to us. Sure enough, at least one always came and landed, even if only briefly. It took a little more practice for my youngest son to develop this ability. He was always a little impatient with himself and the animals. Eventually he learned to calm his mind and emotions and he discovered that when he did so, the animals would respond.

One summer, I had an invasion of black ants in my home. I told these ants that they did not belong inside the house, that they had all the space they could possibly want outside, and that they were not welcome in my home because it was my domain. I also told them that if they insisted on coming inside, they would die. I will admit to feeling a little silly, but it worked-they left! I was also relieved because I really did not want to kill them; they were just ants being ants after all.

After my mother died, her cat, Tigger, came to live with me. He settled in but never seemed happy. (He always had a somewhat grumpy disposition!) Tigger was an old guy, and I was worried about him. Alice was a classmate of mine and was working toward being an animal communicator. She agreed to try to talk with Tigger.

Tigger told Alice he was confused. He didn't understand what had happened. One minute he had been living with his (my) mom, and the next thing he knew, he was at my house. Living at my house was okay, and he liked the dog that looked like him. He also said he liked being able to eat in the windowsill so he could look outside.

I was blown away. Alice and Tigger had never met. He was an orange tabby cat, and my golden shepherd mix was the dog he was referring to. I would put his food dish in the windowsill so he could eat undisturbed and without fear the dogs would eat his food. It had never occurred to me to tell Tigger what had happened to my mom, his owner. I now know better. Whenever I know of an animal whose owner has died, I share this story and encourage the new family to tell the animal what happened. I'd also like to mention that should you have a household with more than one pet and one of them dies, tell the others what happened.

Late one Saturday afternoon, I encountered an older white hound dog in a park near my home. The dog appeared to be lost. He was dirty, walked with a limp, and was tired. His tongue was hanging out of his mouth and he was panting. It seemed he may have been wandering for some time. I looked around the park for a possible owner and saw no one in sight. I lived only a few miles away, so I put the dog in my car, took him home and gave him some food and water. On the way to my house, I asked the dog his name, and I heard the reply, "Ollie."

I decided that if I were unable to locate Ollie's owner over the weekend, I would place an ad in the local newspaper on Monday morning, in hopes of reuniting him with his family. Throughout the weekend, I walked and drove Ollie around the neighborhood, hoping to find a clue as to who he belonged to. I found nothing, not even a "LOST DOG" sign posted to a telephone pole. I placed the ad.

A few days later, I received a phone call from a woman who thought Ollie might be her father's dog. Ollie and I went to the address the woman gave me, which was about eight blocks away from my house. Sure enough, "Taco" belonged to her father, Ole!

It was after their reunion that I realized we'd driven past Taco's house several times. He had whimpered each time we drove by it, but I wasn't very tuned into him and completely missed his cue!

THOUGHTS FOR CONSIDERATION:

- What animals are you drawn to? Have your "favorites" changed over the course of your life?
- Which animals do you have an aversion to? Did something happen to cause this?
- What do you feel their lessons are for you?
- What have they taught you? What else can they teach you?

- When an animal presents itself, what are its attributes or qualities that reflect you, your life, or present circumstances? Has the animal shown up alone or in a group and is this behavior atypical?

Additional Ways to Use Your Psychic Abilities

SPIRIT WILL USE YOUR natural talents and gifts to help convey their messages if you are willing to allow it. Here are additional ways to be of service to those living and in the spirit world.

Medical Intuitive/Healer – Healing is one of the gifts of the Spirit mentioned in the book of Corinthians II in the Bible, and we are all capable of being healers. It's innate within us. ALL healing comes from Creator – God – Spirit – Universe, or whatever you choose to call it. As a healer, you act as a witness and a conduit in the healing process.

As a medical intuitive or body/energy worker, it is useful to have a basic understanding of anatomy and how the body works, as well as becoming skilled at reading auras and chakras. My psychic abilities added immeasurably to my reflexology practice and my ability to assist my clients. You will find suggestions for channel healing at the end of the book.

A word of caution: by law, unless you are a licensed doctor, you are not allowed to diagnose, treat, or prescribe. Check for additional requirements and ordinances in your municipality.

Locating Lost Items – There was an occasion when I was asked to see if I could locate an important piece of missing jewelry for a client. I psychically saw emerald green and heard the tune, "For He's a Jolly Good Fellow" in my psychic ear. I had the sense of feeling animated and almost giddy, like I was at a fun party having a really good time. I passed this information on to the client, and stated I felt she'd find the jewelry near or behind something like a cup and saucer or a plate.

A few days later, the missing piece of jewelry was found. It was in an emerald green velvet bag sitting on a shelf in the china cabinet. The client had set it down on the shelf as she was preparing for a party at her home. The guests sang, "For SHE'S a Jolly Good Fellow" to her.

In addition to using your psychic skills to find a lost item, ask the item to reveal its location to you.

Finding Missing Persons or Working with the Police – Should this be the road you wish to travel, you must be **very** sure of your psychic abilities and even then, proceed with caution. This type of work is not television entertainment.

You will undoubtedly see some horrific, disturbing, and very heartbreaking and graphic images.

Most of the time, psychic information will be received as snapshots or snippets of information such as a lake surrounded by pine trees or a tall, grey building, all of which are pieces of a psychic puzzle but not an entire picture. Typically, the information will not make sense except in hindsight.

Unless you can give a very specific description and include an address or an exact location (corner of 5th and Main in Anytown), your information, however well-meaning, will not be welcomed by the authorities. Even if the information you receive is specific, it will most likely be met with suspicion and skepticism, and rightly so. When a person goes missing, there is an influx of psychics who call the police giving them "helpful hints."

Do **NOT** go to the police announcing you are psychic and stating you can help them solve cases. Should you develop a propensity for solving missing persons cases or other crimes, your reputation as a psychic will speak for itself and the police will come to you.

It should also be noted that if you become too good at solving missing persons cases or other crimes, you may be looked upon as a suspect.

Sadly, our daily newsfeed is filled with missing individuals and unsolved crimes. Here is a way to practice. Keep a notebook dedicated to finding missing persons. When an individual is missing or a crime is committed, record your impressions. Use your psychic senses to discern who, what, where, when, and how. Get as much detail as you can. Follow the case to the end.

Medium Alyson Gannon (www.SpiritCommunication.com) facilitates excellent classes on becoming a psychic detective as well as other classes.

Grief Management – The main responsibilities of a medium are to provide comfort and show that life exists beyond that which we know as death. Additional training with an organization such as Hospice may help you provide this service.

Regardless of the path your intuition or psychic abilities take you:

- Stay true to yourself.
- Always maintain your integrity.
- Honor the work.
- Keep learning.
- Practice, practice, practice.

I sincerely hope you enjoyed this book and found the exercises and activities useful. If you would like to host a workshop in your area, contact me. I'd love to come and play!!!

STEPS TO CHANNELING A HEALING

1. Ground and center yourself.

2. Clear the healing space by smudging, saying a prayer, or envisioning healing light and energy filling the space before your client arrives.

3. Ask the client what they need healing for and ask if they are okay with touch. Never touch the client's genital area or breasts, or any other area where the client states they feel vulnerable. For instance, I know many individuals who are very uncomfortable having hands placed near their throat.
If the client is unable to interact (perhaps comatose or physically distant), ask permission of their Higher Self or soul. Respect the decision given because the answer may be no!

4. While the client gets comfortable on a massage table or in a chair, prepare yourself by washing your hands and/or saying a quick prayer or mantra. Feel healing energy flow into your hands.

5. Ask Universe (or God/Creator/Spirit) to clear your client's body, mind, and soul, and to open your client to receive healing.

6. Ask the Universe to clear **you**, and **you**r body, mind, and soul, and ask the Universe to work through you as a channel for the healing energy.

7. Lay your hands lightly on or just above the client. Listen to your inner voice for guidance to proceed.

8. You may wish to move your hands in circles over your client to prepare your client's body to receive healing.

9. Listen to your hands and intuition throughout the healing session, channeling energy for 20-40 minutes or however long you feel guided to work.

10. When you are finished channeling healing, place your hands about 5 or 6 inches above your client's body. With the left hand, go in a clockwise circle and with the right hand, a counterclockwise circle simultaneously, connecting the circles together. Repeat this on all the areas you channeled energy into. This is like placing a spiritual bandage on the area(s) that have been worked on. Again, listen to your intuition on this.

11. Beginning at the client's head, run your hands (still 5-6 inches above the body) straight down over the body, and down to the feet. This is smoothing or brushing the aura and should be done three to four times.

12. Silently express gratitude for your clients' healing and the opportunity to participate in it. Remember it is not YOUR healing energy, but that of the Universe. You are simply the conduit. Clear yourself, your body, mind, and spirit, your table or chair, and the healing space.

13. Wash your hands and drink some water.

14. Energy work is powerful, and your client may feel disoriented after a session. Encourage them to take their time reorienting themselves. You may offer them some water as well.

15. If you choose to do distant healing, follow these same steps. You may also use something as a surrogate to step in as a substitute for your client. I use a stuffed dog named Ralph.

16. You are not responsible for the outcome.

House Clearing and
Cleansing Procedure

HOUSE CLEARING AND CLEANSING can be done
quickly and simply. Here are a few easy steps to follow.

1. Start with your intention. Do you want your home to feel
peaceful, calm, loving? How do you want it to feel?

2. Choose a prayer such as The Lord's Prayer or the Prayer
of Protection, a mantra such as *"My house is filled with Light
and Love,"* or something else meaningful to you that will indicate your intention.

3. Activate your palm energy centers and, with your palms
facing away from you in a "STOP" position, go from room
to room, speaking your chosen words. Feel the power of your
words and the energy of Spirit flowing out from your hands,
filling the entire room from ceiling to floor. Don't forget the
closets!

4. Should you wish, you may also light a smudge stick, incense, or candle, or spray Florida water in each room to assist with the cleansing. Envision the smoke or mist filling, clearing, and cleansing each room, including the attic and basement.

5. Feel each room you enter becoming filled with love, peace, and serenity, or whatever intention you have chosen.

6. When you have completed this procedure, take some time for gratitude, and give thanks.

Mary Ann Winkowski has a fantastic negative energy releasement protocol you can follow in her book, *When Ghosts Speak*.

THE LORD'S PRAYER

Our Father, who art in heaven
Hallowed be thy name.
Thy kingdom come,
Thy will be done, on earth as it is in heaven.
Give us this day our daily bread
And forgive us our trespasses, as we forgive those who
trespass against us.
And lead us not into temptation but deliver us from evil.
For thine is the kingdom and the power and the glory,
forever. Amen

PRAYER OF PROTECTION* by James Dillet Freeman

The Light of God surrounds me
The Love of God enfolds me
The Power of God protects me
The Presence of God watches over me
Wherever I am, God is
And all is well. Amen

(*This is a shortened version of the original, but one I
always use.)

FIELD NOTES

THE FOLLOWING FIELD NOTE pages may assist you in recording and making notations of your observations and findings in your healings, investigations, and readings. Copy them if you desire.

If you are seeing clients for healings, they can be useful to refer to so you can track your client's progress. It also will help remind you of areas that might require additional healing for future sessions.

If you are doing paranormal investigations, making notations about your investigations are important. You may be able to validate some findings immediately, but other information may come later. For example: I once did an investigation and before I got to the location, energetically saw a house with green asphalt shingle siding. When I arrived, the house had white siding. I later learned it had been originally sided with green asphalt shingles.

Give completed aura and psychic reading pages to the client. You really have no reason to keep them.

As always, be mindful of confidentiality.

AURA READINGS

Have your tools (paper, pens, colored pencils, etc.) ready before you begin.

As you observe your client's aura, notice the colors and their vibrancy within the aura, and where the colors are located. Are there breaks or scarring in the aura? What other information can you gather?

Draw your findings freestyle or use the following template (or draw a stick figure!) to record them.

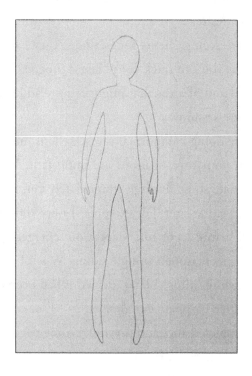

PSYCHIC SESSION IMPRESSIONS AND NOTES

Date:

Name of Sitter:

Sitters' Request(s) or Question(s):

What psychic images present themselves? What are you seeing? Be as detailed as you can.

Colors? Sounds? Tastes? Smells?

Do you get feelings or sensations anywhere on your body? What are they?

What message or messages do you have for your sitter?

Do you make a referral and if so, to whom?

PARANORMAL INVESTIGATION NOTES

Date:

Contact:

Location:

Do you have previous knowledge of this location? If so, what do you know about it?

What are your psychic impressions before you arrive?

What psychic impressions do you get on site?

List and date any validations.

ENERGY FIELD SCANNING NOTES

Name:

Date/Time/Location:

Observations:

Root

Sacral

Solar Plexus

Heart

Thymus

Throat

Third Eye

Crown

How did the client's overall energy feel?

Validations

REFERENCES

Astrology
Seiler, Julie - www.solesthatheal-newageservices.com
Silver, Dawn - www.dawnsilver.com

Auragraphs
Morris, Angie J - www.angiejmorris.com

Essential Oils - www.amrita.net

Ethics
Leath, Melissa/Psychic Integrity - www.melissaleath.com

Healing
Bodine, Echo/Hands that Heal - www.echobodine.com

Intuition
Bodine, Echo - www.echobodine.com
A Still, Small Voice & The Gift
Ko, Lisa/Intuition on Demand - www.lmk88.com

Metaphysical Studies
Michelle, Tina - www.tinamichelle.com

Numerology
Baughman, Alison - www.visiblebynumbers.com

Paranormal Investigation
Conder, Kathy/Michigan Paranormal Encounters
MPEncounterskathy@gmail.com
Kaczmarek, Dale - www.ghostresearch.org

Psychics/Mediums
Bodine, Echo - www.echobodine.com
Gannon, Alyson - www.SpiritCommunication.com
John, Thomas - www.mediumthomasjohn.com
Michelle, Tina - www.tinamichelle.com
Nohavec, Janet - www.janetnohavec.com
Pattilla, Mavis - www.mavispittilla.com
Van Praagh, James - www.vanpraagh.com
Winkowski, Mary Ann - www.maryannwinkowski.com

Learning Centers
Arthur Findlay College - www.arthurfindlaycollege.org
Center for Intuitive Living - www.echobodine.com
House of the Spirit - www.houseofthespirit.org
Lily Dale - www.lilydaleassembly.org

Morris Pratt Institute - www.morrispratt.org

Viva Institute - www.vivainstitute.com

ADDITIONAL METAPHYSICAL BOOKS YOU MAY ENJOY:

Baughman, Alison

Speaking to Your Soul Through Numerology

Bodine, Echo

A Still, Small Voice - Echoes of the Soul - Look for the Good and You'll Find God

My Big Book of Healing - Relax, It's Only a Ghost - What Happens When We Die?

The Gift: Understand and Develop Your Psychic Abilities

John, Thomas

Never Argue with a Dead Person

Kaczmarek, Dale D.

Field Guide to Ghost Hunting Techniques - Field Guide to Spirit Photography

Ko, Lisa

Intuition on Demand

Kardec, Allan

The Spirits' Book - The Mediums' Book

Leath, Melissa

Psychic Integrity

Nohavec, Janet

Through the Darkness - Where Two Worlds Meet

Van Praagh, James

Talking to Heaven: A Medium's Message of Life after
Death

Unfinished Business: What the Dead Can Teach Us
About Life

Winkowski, Mary Ann

When Ghosts Speak

IMPORTANT PHONE NUMBERS
TO HAVE AVAILABLE

National Alliance on Mental Illness (NAMI)

1.800.950.6264 (NAMI)

National Domestic Violence Helpline

1.800.700.7233 (SAFE)

National Drug Helpline

1.844.289.0879 (Alcohol Addiction)

National Sexual Assault Hotline

1.800.656.4673 (HOPE)

National Suicide Prevention Lifeline

1.800.273.8255

Substance Abuse & Mental Health

Service Administration (SAMHSA)

1.800.662.4357 (HELP)

Be sure to have your local numbers available as well.

Made in United States
North Haven, CT
02 June 2024

53234785R00114